The Wrath and Judgments of God

Don T. Phillips

"The Wrath and Judgments of God," by Don T. Phillips. ISBN 978-1-63868-109-0.

Published 2023 by Virtualbookworm.com Publishing Inc., P.O. Box 9949, College Station, TX 77845, US. Copyright ©2023 Don T. Phillips.

All rights reserved. No part of this publication may be reproduced, stored in a retrieval system, or transmitted in any form or by any means, electronic, mechanical, recording or otherwise, without the prior written permission of Don T. Phillips.

Dedication

This book is dedicated to:

Philip Blackburn

And

Weldon Mackey

Christian Brothers

and

Real Men

Preface

This book is intended to examine, explain and discuss Jehovah God as a *God of Wrath* and righteous character. There are few Biblical topics that cause a Christian to withdraw and disengage from a typical, modern Christian theology than a discussion of the *Wrath of God*. the average Christian does not want to even consider that a righteous, loving God can also be a vengeful, God of Wrath.

Most Pastors and few theologians will teach about or discuss the Wrath of God, but the Biblical Truth of God's eternal plan for mankind will ultimately end in the Wrath of God being apportioned to every person who has not believed in Jesus Christ as the Son of God and as the final and perfect sacrifice for all sins. The Wrath of God is for sinners and not true believers

He that believeth on the Son hath everlasting life: and he that believeth not the Son shall not see life; but the Wrath of God abides on him   John 3:36

According to Webster, *wrath* is strong, vengeful anger. This definition might explain a *motive* for anger but it does not explain the *motivation*. In the Holy Scriptures, wrath is always defined as the anger of God towards man. The motivation for God's anger is can always be traced to *sin* and *disobedience*. God is holy, perfect and truthful in every way and cannot tolerate sin. God may not immediately react and judge sinful actions and behavior, but He can never forget or forgive sinful behavior.

If God is holy and righteous and cannot tolerate sin, how can sinful man ever hope to achieve righteousness or eternal life in God's kingdom? When God created the earth, He placed a sinless, perfect man in the Garden of Eden to commune with Him and live in a sinless state forever. He gave man a companion called Eve who was also sinless and was created to keep man company and populate the earth with the seed of Abraham. We all know what happened: Lucifer tempted Eve with forbidden fruit, and she committed the first sinful act of disobedience against God by eating fruit from the tree of knowledge of good and evil. Rather than bear her trespass alone, she persuaded Adam to also eat of the forbidden fruit. Sin is always destructive and has no bounds. Satan is a lier and the father of all lies. Through the disobedience and sinful act of one man, sin entered the world. The perfect and holy Garden of Eden was no longer suitable for sinful man, and so God had no choice but to remove them from a sinless world and place them in a sinful world. Sin and disobedience always extract a heavy price.

Even as God judged and sentenced Adam and Eve to physical death in an imperfect world, He already had a plan to redeem His creation and restore man to a sinless state. It should be obvious that since man was now a sinful and imperfect creature, there was no way to transform his sinful nature and sinful flesh to a perfect man. The solution would not be a physical transformation but a spiritual transformation. Since God cannot tolerate or forgive sin, He sent Jesus Christ to a sinful world to forgive all sins. The imperfect body of sinful man would die, but the soul of man…. who is perfect…. lives on forever. Jesus Christ was God born into the flesh by a virgin woman (Mother Mary) and lived a perfect life. He never sinned…He never broke one of God's commandments or laws and He offered Himself as the sinless, Lamb of God who was sacrificed for all of the sins of sinful man. In order to receive this gift only one requirement was necessary: Each individual must believe in faith that Jesus Christ lived and died as the Son of God, and that justification of sinful man to stand forgiven in the presence of God is by the Blood of Jesus Christ. The spiritual transformation of sinful man was by being born-again by simple faith that Jesus Christ was God in the flesh and died for our sins. What a wonderful and flawless plan for the redemption of mankind! When every sinful man or woman finds themselves standing before the Throne of God there will be only one question that will be asked; *What did you do with my Son Jesus Christ?* If the answer is simply: *I trusted His word and believe that He died for my sins……*God will simply say: *Enter into the Kingdom of God forever.* Sadly, there is another answer to the one question that God will ask: *I did not believe that your Son died for my sins.* God will have no choice but to answer: *Depart from me into a place called the Lake of Burning Fire…..* **I do not know you and I never knew you.**

The eternal plan of God to redeem mankind started when Adam and Eve were both cast out of the Garden of Eden, and will end when the Great White Throne Judgment takes place, the earth is renovated by fire and the sinless state of the Garden of Eden is restored. In order to Understand the Wrath of God, it is necessary to understand that the entire history and evolution of mankind has been divided into 7 distinct periods of time called *Dispensations.* These 7 dispensations of time have been further subdivided into 2 distinct periods: (1) The Old Testament and (2) The New Testament. A description of how God dealt with man and a history of events which either have or will take place have been compiled into 66 different *books*: 39 books which collectively describe the Old Testament and 27 books in the New Testament. The Wrath of God can only be understood if it is recognized that in the Old Testament, even during the period of the kings, God ruled over mankind in a *Theocracy*: He was and still is the sovereign and sole ruler over all creation, but for about 4000 years he ruled and reigned. As sovereign ruler, all kings and kingdoms existed at His discretion.

The earth is the LORD's, and the fulness thereof; the world, and they that dwell therein   Psalms 24:1

As sovereign ruler over all nations and kings, God also had the right to pass judgment upon man and to exercise His Righteous Indignation and His Wrath. Until God gave the 10 Commandments and over 113 civil and religious commandments to the Nation of Israel at Mt. Sinai through His servant Moses, the laws and commands were all verbal or existed within the heart of man. After the Law was given at Mt. Sinai, a written set of rules by which to live were given to man. Even though a set of written laws were given to man at Mt. Sinai, mankind was still directly responsible to God as sovereign ruler. The only change was that before Mt. Sinai there were only verbal laws from God and after Mt. Sinai there were written laws. In either case. Violation of the written or unwritten laws of God was a sin, and God could respond to any transgressions with righteous indignation or the Wrath of God. In the Old Testament, sin and transgression against the Laws of God could be temporarily overlooked or immediately dealt with. In either case, sin will never go unnoticed or forgiven in the Old Testament. As we study the Wrath of God in the Old Testament, payment for sins and transgression was often immediate and deadly.

God punished sin in the Old Testament whenever his rules and Laws were violated. Between Adam and Eve and the *Dispensation of Innocence* until God gave the Law to the Nation of Israel at Mt. Sinai, and He initiated the *Dispensation of The Law*, there were no written laws. Whatever laws were personally enforced by God and the Wrath of God which followed disobedience, we have little or no record. Of course, we know from the Holy Scriptures *what* God did to those who broke His unwritten laws. After the *Written Law* was given at Mt. Sinai, mankind became worse and worse until it became obvious to God that no one could be saved under any set of verbal or written laws. If mankind was to be saved and a sinless earth restored, a new and completely different plan needed to be implemented. This plan was to send a Messiah and a redeemer named *Jesus Christ*, the *Son of God*, to forgive the sins of man…past, present and future. Jesus Christ was that long-awaited messiah who lived a sinless, perfect life and then offered Himself as the final and complete sacrifice for all sins. *Under the Law*, God had chosen only the Nation of Israel to be his peculiar, chosen people. There were only two classes of people: Jews and gentiles. **The term *gentile* describes every person of non-Jewish heritage.** The Old Testament often describes the gentiles as people who worship other gods. Gentiles were all excluded from the commonwealth of God. When Christ came to redeem sinful man, the written law was replaced by laws and precepts which were written on the heart. On the Cross of Calvary, Jesus Christ shed His blood for the sins of the world, and salvation was offered to all mankind…. Jews and gentiles alike.

The great dividing line between all mankind is the Cross of Calvary. The division between the Old Testament and the New Testament marks a significant change in the way that the Wrath of God is administered to mankind. In the Old Testament, there are numerous times when God released His Wrath upon individuals or groups of individuals for sins and disobedience. One will search in vain for even one display of Gods Wrath in the New Testament until the Church Age comes to an end. At that time there will be several corporate judgments on mankind which will be either for believers (rewards) or unbelievers (punishment). Obviously, a dramatic change in how the Wrath of God is executed. There are only two occasions when anger was displayed in the New Testament, and both did not lead to destruction or death…. both happened on the same day. Christ was about to be betrayed and crucified, and early one morning He entered Jerusalem to teach and heal in the temple. As He passed a fig tree, Jesus was hungry and turned to a fig tree to eat its fruit, but He found that the tree was barren of fruit. In a rare act of anger, Christ cursed the tree and it withered away to the roots (Matthew 21: 18-24). This rare incident was not just to highlight the humanity of Christ, but it was a sign unto the Jews. They had been offered redemption by the Messiah but they rejected Him and had made plans for His betrayal and crucifixion. This act of unbelief and rejection by the corporate Jews and the religious leaders of the Jews would have far-reaching effects. After the Jews were *first* offered forgiveness of sins and salvation by Christ at the Day of Pentecost and Steven was stoned in Jerusalem, Jesus Christ would be sent by God to anoint Paul as the person who would go to the Gentiles. After the Cross of Calvary, salvation and forgiveness of sins would be offered by faith and grace to both Jews and gentiles. From that point on, mankind would be divided into only two groups once again: Believers and unbelievers.

This dramatic change was always apart of God' eternal plan to redeem all mankind and offer His eternal kingdom to those who would believe. The agent for this dramatic change was His son Jesus Christ. The *plan* for salvation was known to God since time began, but the *executer* of that plan was our Lord Jesus Christ.

Jesus was the fulfillment of the Old Testament Jewish traditions and roles. Jesus does not simply represent a new way of doing things. Rather, He is supreme. He is the actual fulfillment of the old way of doing things and is therefore greater than those ways. Concerning the temple system under the Mosaic Law, the author of Hebrews writes: .. *But now hath he obtained a more excellent ministry, by how much also he is the mediator of a better covenant, which was established upon better promises* (Hebrews 8:6)Jesus is greater than the Old Testament systemin every way. He both encompasses and supersedes the old way of doing things. This is evident in the many comparisons of Jesus to Old Testament roles and rituals. For instance, we are told that: *because Jesus lives forever, he has a permanent priesthood. Therefore, he is able to save completely those who come to God through him, because he always lives to intercede for them* (Hebrews 7:24–25). Jesus encompasses the Old Testament priesthood and is supreme over it

> Because Jesus is supreme, this excludes us from saying that He is only one of many ways to God. He is not just a good moral teacher whom we may choose to follow; rather, He is God, and He is over all. Jesus' supremacy also makes it evident that we cannot atone for our own sins. In fact: *It is impossible for the blood of bulls and goats to take away sins* (Hebrews 10:4). Jesus both fulfilled and replaced any and all Old Testament systems. Salvation is not based on works (Ephesians 2:1–10). Jesus is preeminent and is now exhalated over all things. The supremacy of Jesus teaches us that He is not simply a spiritual being above the rest. Paul tells us that through Him all things visible and invisible, in heaven and on earth.   Extracted from **Got Questions?**

Part of the supremacy of Jesus is that since He suffered and died on the Cross of Calvary, and then ascended to heaven as the Firstfruits of all creation He is worthy to judge those who dwell upon the earth: Believers and unbelievers. Scripture reveals that it will be God the Son who will be the ultimate judge of humanity. He has the qualifications to be the righteous judge. This is why there are no direct acts of Wrath by God the Father found between the Book of Matthew and the Book of Revelation. There will be judgments and Wrath against mankind but not until the *Dispensation of Grace* and the Millennial Dispensation has ended has ended. This book will summarize and present the *Wrath of God* from *Adam* to the *Great White Throne Judgment.*

Chapter 1: God's Plan for the Fullness of Time
Chapter 2: Judgment and the Wrath of God
Chapter 3: Judgments and the Wrath of God in the *Old Testament*
Chapter 4: Judgments and the Wrath of God in the *New Testament*

The Authorized King James Bible will be used for all Scriptural Quotations.

Don T. Phillips
January 2023

Table of Contents

Chapter 1: God's Plan for the Fulness of Time 1
   The Dispensations of God 2
   The Issue of Sin 3
   The Eternal Plan of God and the 7 Dispensations 4
      Dispensation of Innocence 5
      Dispensation of Conscience 6
      Dispensation of Man's Rule 7
      Dispensation of New Beginnings 10
         The Age of Promise 10
         The Age of Bondage 11
      Dispensation of the Law 11
      Dispensation of Grace 12
      The Millennial Dispensation 13
   The Covenants of God 14
      Conditional Covenants 15
      Unconditional Covenants 16
     The 8 Covenants Between God and Man 17
      Edenic Covenant 17
      Adamic Covenant 18
      Noahidic Covenant 18
      Abrahamic Covenant 18
      Mosaic Covenant 20
      Davidic Covenant 20
      Covenant of Grace 21
      Millennial Covenant 22
     Promise of the Land 23

Chapter 2: Judgment and the Wrath of God 29
   Three Different Types of Judgment 34
   Righteous Judgment and the Wrath of God 36

  The Righteousness of God 42

Chapter 3: Judgments and Wrath of God in the Old Testament 45

  The Dateless Past: The Fallen Angels 46

  The Dispensation of Innocence 49

  The Dispensation of Conscience 50

    Adam and Eve 52

    The Nephilim 58

    Cain and Abel 60

    Gods Wrath Upon Mankind: *Noah and the Great Flood* 63

  The Dispensation of Man's Rule 67

    Nimrod and the Tower of Babel 67

    Sodom and Gomorrah 69

  The Dispensation of New Beginnings 71

    What Was Israel Doing in Egypt? 75

    The Wrath of God: *Israel in Egyptian Bondage* 75

    Moses is Chosen by God 79

      Liberating Israel from Egyptian Slavery: *The 10 Plagues* 83

      The Wrath of God: *Red Sea Crossing* 86

  The Dispensation of Law 89

    Aaron and the Golden Calf 91

    Korah's Rebellion 95

    Nadab and Abihu 93

    Miriam and Her Complaints 98

    Joshua and the Ten Spies 100

    The Wrath of God: *Moses and Aaron* 101

    Jannes and Jambes 104

    The Conquest of Jericho 104

      Achan and the Wrath of God 105

        The Wrath of God: *Destroys the Enemies of Joshua* 107

        The Reign of King David 108

    Fall of the Northern Kingdom 109

    Fall of the Southern Kingdom 110

Chapter 4: Judgments and Wrath of God in the *New Testament*.. *114*

    The Dispensation of Grace 114

    The *Wilderness Rod Judgment* 121

    Judgment of the Nations: *Sheep and Goats* 124

   The Millennial Dispensation 126

    The *Great White Throne Judgment* 126

BIBLIOGRAPHY *130*

Chapter 1
God's Plan for the Fullness of Time

Every Christian should be aware of God's progressive plan to redeem mankind. The plan of God involves 7 *Dispensations of Time*. The word *dispensation* should not confuse or bewilder any Christian today. A *Dispensation of Time* is simply a *finite period of time over which God has dealt or will deal with men in a distinct way to fulfill His redemptive plan.* God created man to be free from sin. This is such an important basic concept that 7 dispensations of time will be briefly reviewed.

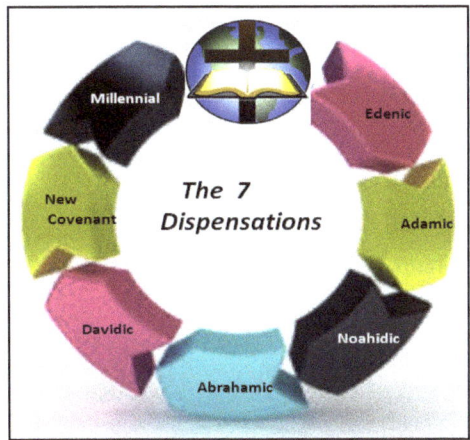

The following graphic will frame our discussion.

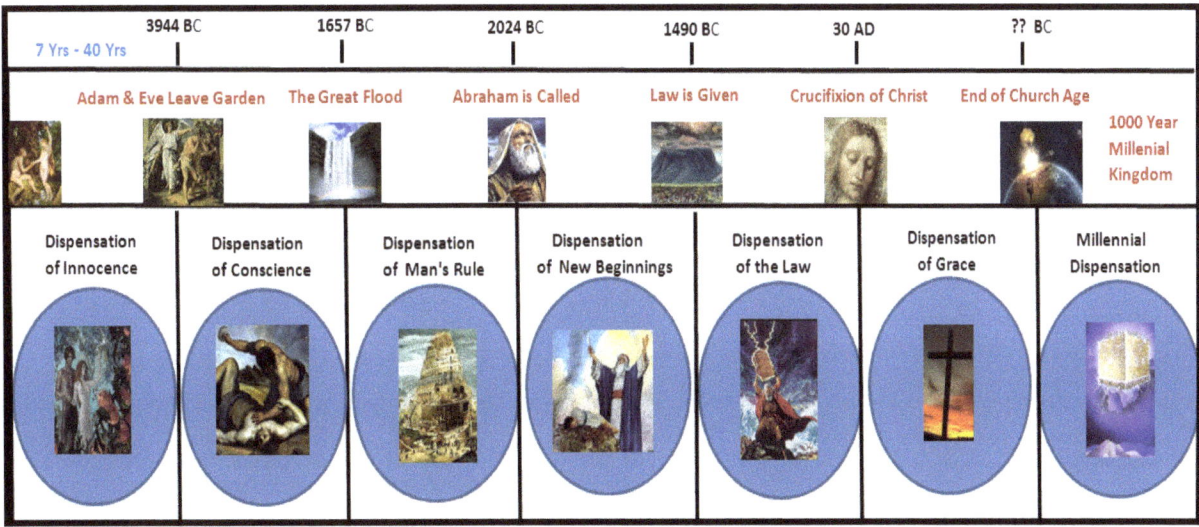

The period of time between when the 1st dispensation started (The Dispensation of Innocence) and the last dispensation ends (The Millennial Dispensation) spans when Adam and Eve were created in the Garden of Eden until the end of the 1000-year Millennial Kingdom. Adam and Eve were created by God to live forever and repopulate the earth (Genesis 1:28a, KJV), and he was to have dominion over the fish of the sea, the fowl of the air, and every other living thing that moved upon the earth (Genesis 1:28b). Adam was created to be the first of a race of humans who would be sinless in the sight of God. God wanted to commune with man, and walk with him in the cool of the evening (Genesis 3:8). However, we all know the story of how Eve was beguiled, deceived by Satan and committed the first sin. Adam and Eve had only one command from God, and that was to never eat from the *Tree of the Knowledge of Good and Evil*, but Satan tempted Eve and she did. She then perpetuated her sin by talking Adam into eating the fruit of this tree also. This was rebellion and the 1st sin against the creator. For their disobedience, they were both condemned to eventual physical death and were expunged from the Garden. This one act of disobedience has cursed man ever since. Since all of the people of this world were spawned from the seed of Adam, man inherited this original sin from Adam and were born with a sin nature. The purpose of God ever since has been to restore man to an original sinless state and once again commune with His creation just as He intended in the beginning. This eternal purpose of God will be accomplished through His Son Jesus Christ. The entire spectrum of man's existence and the reconciliation of mankind will be accomplished when the 7 dispensations of time have been fulfilled. The fullness of time is marked by one holy and eternal watershed…the sacrificial death of Jesus Christ on the Cross of Calvary. This monumental and ordained event was *preceded* by 5 different dispensations and will be *followed* by two other different dispensations of time: *The Church Age* or the Age of Grace and the 1000-year *Millennial Kingdom*.

Dispensations of God

A *dispensation* is defined as a certain *period of time* during which God deals with people in a particular way. The Greek word for dispensation is *oikonomia*, and in the Bible it is used to mean a *manner, method, or particular arrangement of dealing with a group of people that God has chosen.* Defining a dispensation, a fixed period of time will not bear up under close scrutiny of the scriptures. Usually, the length of time is not emphasized or even mentioned; it is the manner in which God is dealing with mankind over a particular period time which distinguishes one dispensation from another. The word **dispensation** is found four times in the scriptures, all in the New Testament writings of the apostle Paul (I Corinthians 9:17, Ephesians 1:10, Ephesians 3:2, Colossians 1:25). Each verse makes it clear that God has always dealt with man according to specific promises, commands, relationship and laws. In Ephesians 3:2, Paul revealed to the Gentiles that God is now redeeming man by *faith* and *grace* and not by *works*. Faith is defined to operate not only over a specific period of time (The Dispensation of Grace), but across all time both before and after the cross. It is not a work-based doctrine but a faith-based doctrine. The salvation of mankind has always been based upon *faith* in His Son, Jesus Christ, and is a free gift. The Old Testament saints from Adam to the 1st advent of Jesus Christ only knew that forgiveness of sins and redemption would someday come by a prophesied redeemer; New Covenant saints now know that the *anointed* or *appointed* one was *Jesus Christ*. Salvation by faith has *always* been the only way that mankind could be redeemed from sin. In reality, it was not free at all but a great price was paid by Jesus Christ for the redemption of all mankind on the cross of Calvary.

The *Dispensation of Grace* can be contrasted with the *Dispensation of the Law,* where the relationship between man and God was based upon observing God's written laws. Under the Law, obedience was not an option but was demanded by God. Obey the laws and live; break them and die (Galatians 3:10-13). The Law only condemned and was put in place to show people that it was impossible to live under God's standards. There were at least 113 different commands by God which defined the Law, and James wrote that if one breaks only one law, he has broken them all.

For whosoever shall keep the whole law, and yet offend in one point, he is guilty of all   James 2:10

The Issue of Sin

For all have sinned, and come short of the glory of God   Romans 3:23

The opposite of *death* is *life*, and Jesus Christ came not to abolish the law as a means to obtain eternal life, but to replace the law with a New Covenant that is based upon salvation by faith and grace. Salvation by works under the law was replaced by salvation by faith and grace, and this new dispensation was initiated and ratified by the atoning work of Jesus Christ upon the Cross. Although the law was finished as a means to obtain eternal life, the 10 Commandments of God which was given to the Jews at Mt. Sinai was not annulled or replaced. The 10 commandments were given by God and they were and still are holy.

the law is holy, and the commandment holy, and just, and good   Romans 7:10

In the *Dispensation of the New Covenant,* the law is still holy and good because it was given to man by God, who is pure and good.... but if any one law is violated or broken, it no longer condemns man to spiritual death. Christ said: *I am the way, the truth and the life.* It is not that the Law was unjust: Salvation by grace does not negate the law, but makes it possible for all who believe in Jesus Christ as their savior to live, and not die, under eternal condemnation.

For the law having a shadow of good things to come, and not the very image of the things, can never with those sacrifices which they offered year by year continually make the comers thereunto perfect.   Hebrews 10:1

When Christ died on the Cross of calvary, He declared: *It is finished.* He was not merely declaring that His earthly ministry was finished, but that salvation under works of the law were finished: The Levitical sacrificial system and temporary atonement for sins were finished: The barrier which separated the Jews and Gentiles was finished; Salvation by works was replaced by salvation by faith and grace: And the issue of sin as a barrier to eternal life was finished. Christ was the perfect sacrificial Lamb of God whose blood was offered as the complete, perfect and final sacrifice for all sins…past, present and future.

Knowing that a man is not justified by the works of the law, but by the faith of Jesus Christ, even we have believed in Jesus Christ, that we might be justified by the faith of Christ, and not by the works of the law: for by the works of the law shall no flesh be justified.   Galatians 2:16

The Eternal Plan of God and the 7 Different Dispensations

God uses dispensations to deal with man in different ways, under different circumstances, to teach and reveal Himself and His eternal plan. When God reveals himself to man, the revelation may be at a specific point in time; but because it is the nature and character of God that is being revealed it is usually not bound to that particular point in time or necessarily limited to the dispensation in which it is revealed

The rest of this chapter will provide an overview of the seven different dispensations that will span the existence of mankind upon this earth. We will then identify and discuss 24 different points in time that God has executed righteous judgment against mankind, and 3 judgments which are yet to take place. God and man are currently in the 6th dispensation of time, and it has been almost 6000 years since Adam and Eve were created.

Dispensation of Innocence

The *Disposition of Innocence* began with the creation of Adam and Eve and continued until they sinned against God and were cast out of the Garden of Eden. The duration of this period of time is unknown. It has been proposed as one week, less than one year, seven years and even 40 years long by various biblical scholars. The end of the Dispensation of Innocence clearly demonstrates what can happen to man if he follows his own will and conscience and fails to obey a sovereign and Holy God.

When Adam and Eve were cast out of the Garden of Eden, they left a perfect, sinless place. They were given dominion over all of the earth and were nourished by all manners of fruit which grew in the Garden. They were only required to till and keep the Garden of Eden in which they lived, and to replenish the earth with their offspring. The concept of sin was not known at all. God had only one command or law, and that was that Adam or Eve could not partake (eat) of the fruit of the *Tree of Good and Evil*. When Lucifer came and tempted them to eat the fruit of the *Knowledge of Good and Evil*, he told Eve a lie which she believed. Satan convinced Eve that if she ate the fruit, she would not die but knowing good from evil she would then be like God. Eve's problem was the same as men and women have today; she thought that she knew more than God. We should not be strictly critical of Eve; Adam ate the fruit also. So, both Adam and Eve sinned by eating the fruit and for that sin they were expunged from the Garden of Eden. They would have lived forever and walked with God in the cool of the evening (Genesis 3:8), but from the moment that they both sinned they began to die

(Genesis 2:17). Adam lived for 930 years after he and Eve were cast out of the Garden.

Disposition of Conscience

The *Dispensation of Conscience* lasted about 1,656 years from the time that Adam and Eve were evicted from the Garden of Eden until the Great Flood (Genesis 3:8–8:22). This dispensation of time had no written laws and the behavior of man was dictated by his own will and conscience. This does not imply that man did not know good from evil or was not aware that man did not know sin. The heart and mind of man clearly understood what was right from wrong. Discernment and truth were inherited from Adam when he ate from the tree of knowledge which differentiated good from evil. However: *When there is no written law then how could sin be defined?* (Romans 4:15). The apostle Paul addressed this question when he spoke of the Gentiles, who were not under the law of Moses

[14] *For when the Gentiles, which have not the law, do by nature the things contained in the law, these, having not the law, are a law unto themselves:*
[15] *Which shew the work of the law written in their hearts, their conscience also bearing witness, and their thoughts the mean while accusing or else excusing one another*   Romans 2: 14-15

Every man and woman are inherently aware of good and evil. Each possesses a clear standard by which individual actions can be judged. This understanding and knowledge of good and evil is called *conscience*. Conscience might be the most sensitive aspect of human nature. It is the instinctive knowledge of right from wrong.

Adam was alive during most of this dispensation. He and Eve began to populate the world and live in it. Many things changed when they sinned and were forced to leave the Garden of Eden. Houses had to be built... gardens had to be planted and cultivated... and the animal kingdom was now at enmity against all mankind. In the Garden of Eden, Adam and Eve were vegetarians. Now they could eat meat but no blood. Adam undoubtedly told his offspring and their children the consequences of sin, but they would not listen. They went their own way and did not obey the Lord. There was no written law, but the scriptures clearly reveal that after Adam and Eve fell, evil and sin was understood without any written law. This is made plain when Cain slew Abel. When God found what he had done, Cain responded by saying: *Am I my brother's keeper?* He knew that he was and he knew that he had sinned when he killed his own brother out of jealously. *How did God respond?* He banished Cain from his presence forever and drove him into the wilderness. One cannot mock God or sin against God without suffering the consequences. Things only got progressively worse until God had enough. The earth was filled with violence, corruption and sin; and so, God told Noah to build an *ark*. After 120 years He would destroy the world with a great flood: *The wages of sin is death*. The only righteous people who would be spared from death were Noah, his 3 sons and their wives...eight in all. After the great flood, the world had been purged from all sinful men and women and was ready to begin anew. *Would things now be different?* Unfortunately, sin still existed in every man... the sin nature had been imputed to all of these 8 people by Adam and would be passed on to all who would later be born by man and women.

Dispensation of Man's Rule

The *Dispensation of Man's Rule* has also been called the *Dispensation of Human Government*. It lasted about 425 years and began when Noah and his family left the Ark after God had brought a great flood upon the whole earth. God looked at His creation and found that only Noah, his three sons and their four wives were worthy of saving. It is true that all mankind sprang from Adam and Eve, but it is equally true that people on the earth today also sprang from Noah and his family. Noah and his sons were once again to re-populate the earth, and they ruled themselves without any written laws. They were ruled by their heart, their own conscience and the inherent conflict between good and evil. When man was left to follow his conscience after Adam and Eve was expelled from the Garden of Eden, they failed miserably. They would not learn to live in righteousness. There is a strange paradox concerning what defined sin before the law was given to Moses. Paul wrote:

Blessed is the man to whom the Lord will not impute sin   Romans 4:8

Because the law worketh wrath: for where no law is, there is no transgression
Romans 4:15

If there was no law before Moses, then how could those people before the law was given be held accountable? There may not have been a written law, but we know for sure that sin existed before the law.

[13] *For until the law sin was in the world: but sin is not imputed when there is no law.*
[14] Nevertheless *death reigned from Adam to Moses, even over them that had not sinned after the similitude of Adam's transgression, who is the figure of him that was to come*   Romans 5: 13-14

This is a very difficult passage of scripture. The *law* which Paul references in Romans 5:13 was the Law given to Moses at Mt. Sinai. Paul concludes that even before the law had been written down, sin was already in the world: *Sin reigned between Adam and Moses*. He then paradoxically states that if there is no law then sin cannot be imputed. His conclusion is not only universal but logical. One cannot break a law when there is no law! But Adam sinned against God when there was no written law so the conclusion is that Adam had broken a law against God that was not written down. The inescapable conclusion is that God had verbally declared what constituted sin in His mind, and that man inherently knew right from wrong without anything being written. This is consistent with the original sin of Adam and Eve. When they ate of the forbidden fruit, they instantly knew the difference between good and evil. Even if man did not sin *after the similitude of Adam*...they did not eat of the forbidden fruit.... the *wages of sin are death* and *death still reigned*.

This is an astounding truth to anyone today who thinks that they can be saved without breaking any of the 10 commandments. Christ stated during His earthly ministry that: **all have sinned**, *and come short of the glory of God* (Romans 3:23). Hence, there are only two possible conclusions: (1) Men, before the law was written on tablets of stone, sinned because their conscience and their actions were contrary to any law...written or unwritten. *Who would deny that before the 10 commandments were written down on stone, murder is a sin?* When Cain slew Abel there was no written law, but He clearly understood that he had both lied to God and that he had sinned against his brother (2) Sin is breaking the Law of God. John said: *Sin is lawlessness* (I John 3:4) Sin is not only a transgression of the law of God, it is sinful behavior against the very nature of God: an unrighteous act. Sin is a deviation from the will of God. It is a form of evildoing since it is in opposition to God's decrees and desires. Sin is not merely a moral and mental deficiency; it is open rebellion and disobedience to what God has declared is right. Since sin *was* present before the Law was given on Mt. Sinai (Romans 5:14), ... then not only did conscience reveal sin to man but God must have revealed to them actions which would constitute sin. Either way... there is one immutable and eternal truth that must be understood: Any person between Adam and the cross who had committed a sin, knew that sin must be forgiven if they were to stand before God and inherit eternal life. The 1st prophetic words concerning Christ were spoken to Satan by God in the Garden of Eden:

[14] *And the LORD God said unto the serpent; Because thou hast done this, thou art cursed above all cattle, and above every beast of the field; upon thy belly shalt thou go, and dust shalt thou eat all the days of thy life:*
[15] *And I will put enmity between thee and the woman, and between thy seed and her seed; it shall bruise thy head, and thou shalt bruise his heel*
Genesis 3: 14-15

After sin entered the world, those who trusted God and followed after his precepts and holiness had to believe in faith that God would provide a way to redeem man from the consequences of sin. All of the Old Covenant *saints died in faith* that a redeemer would arise who would take away their sins. This was prophesied by Job in the ancient Book of Job.

[25] *For I know that my redeemer lives, and that he shall stand at the latter day upon the earth:*
[26] *And though after my skin worms destroy this body, yet in my flesh shall I see*
Job 19: 25-26

I grew up believing that the New Testament was for Christians and the Old Testament was for Jews. And by the way, the majority of both groups believe that! But Jesus, the Jewish Messiah brought both the Old and the New seamlessly together. If that is what Yeshua taught (not to mention the Apostles) and accomplished, how could we ignore or disregard a part of the Bible that is obviously so important? It's impossible to understand the New Testament without a basic understanding of the Old Testament. It is like showing up to the second act of a two-act play, having missed the entire first act.

It is reasonable to assume that all who lived before the Law was given to Israel would know that a redeemer would someday arise. The 10 commandments are sometimes called the *Law of Moses*, but make no mistake about it... it should be properly called *the Law of God as given to the people through Moses*. The key concept is that every person from Adam to the end of the Church Age would be saved in exactly the same way....*by faith.*

It very clear that throughout the Old Testament and the Old Covenant, the way to salvation was the same as under the new covenant… By faith alone, through the grace of God, and in Jesus Christ alone. To prove this, Paul speaks of Abraham, who was saved by faith: *Abraham believed God, and it was credited to him as righteousness* (Romans 4:3). Paul quotes the Old Testament to prove his point… Genesis 15:6. Abraham could not have been saved by keeping the Law, because he lived over 430 years before the Law was given.

Dispensation of New Beginnings

The *Dispensation of Man's Rule* ended when God called Abraham out of Ur to live in the land of the Chaldees. At that time, God started a *new* dispensation called the *Disposition of New Beginnings*. This new dispensation established Israel as God's chosen people who would be berthed through Abraham, and it lasted 430 years between when Abraham was called out of the Chaldees to when God liberated Israel from Egyptian bondage. God then gave the written law to Israel at Mount Sinai. The *Dispensation of New Beginnings* was divided into two distinct periods of time: (1) The *Age of Promise,* and (2) The *Age of Bondage.*

The Age of Promise

The *Age of Promise* lasted exactly 215 years. It began when God called Abram out of Ur of the Chaldees and ended when Abraham took his family to Egypt. God made several covenant promises with Abram and then changed his name to *Abraham* (Genesis 7:15), which means "Father of many nations". This was a new beginning with a new patriarch who had been given a new name. They moved to a land with new promises called the *Land of Canaan.* During this period of time Abraham, his nephew Lot (Genesis 12:5), and the new Nation of Israel grew and prospered. As the herds and flocks of Abraham and Lot grew in size, at some point in time Abraham moved to *Hebron.* At Hebron, the Lord first showed Abraham the land that would belong to his offspring forever (Genesis 13:14–17). The ancient city of Hebron was located approximately 20 miles south of present-day Jerusalem. Hebron is significant in the Bible for a couple of reasons. The city is first mentioned in Genesis 13:18 as the place where Abraham traveled after parting company with his nephew Lot. This continued until God caused a natural disaster to occur which was to test the faith of His new nation. Abraham was a great man of faith (Hebrews 11:8), but just like all mortal men his faith gave way to doubt. In an act of not believing God to sustain and protect His chosen people, Abraham left the land of promise and took his families to Egypt. During the period of time that Abraham and his family lived in Canaan, God dealt with Israel as a *theocracy*. He was the divine ruler who directly communicated with man to reveal His sovereign will. When the Children of Israel left Canaan, they were divinely protected by Joseph. After about 7 years, they became slaves making bricks and cutting rocks for the great pyramids. The sub-age of *Promise* had given way to the sub-age of *Bondage*. Promise and prosperity had given way to servitude and slavery.

The Age of Bondage

The *Age of Bondage* also lasted exactly 215 years (Exodus 12: 40-41). Because of unbelief and failure to accept God as their theocratic ruler in Canaan, the Children of Israel became the property of the Egyptian Pharaoh. Israel spent 215 years in Egypt in slavery under several Egyptian Pharaohs. Finally, God in His mercy heard their cries and sent His servant, *Moses,* to lead them out of bondage. Moses was a very unusual man: As a young child He was adopted into Egyptian royalty and served the Pharaoh for 40 years. After he killed an Egyptian, he fled Egypt and became a lowly Shepard in the Land of Midian for another 40 years. As He was tending sheep at age 80, God appeared to him and called him back to Egypt to free his people from Egyptian slavery. The Dispensation of *New Beginnings* ended after Moses led the Nation of Israel out of Egypt, crossed over the Red Sea, and was given the Law of God at Mount Sinai.

Dispensation of The Law

The *Dispensation of the Law* lasted approximately 1520 years. It began at Mt. Sinai in 1490 BC when Moses and the people were given the 10 Commandments, and ended when Christ suffered and died on the Cross of Calvary in 30 AD. The Dispensation of the Law is often called the *Old Covenant*. When it ended, it was superseded and replaced by the *New Covenant*. The Dispensation of the Law had one major feature: God gave Israel a set of 10 commandments through Moses at Mount Sinai after they had crossed the Red Sea and emerged as a free nation. The 10

Commandments....which are generally referred to as *The Law*.... were given to govern their religious and moral character. Through time, another 613 commandments were given to govern their social, dietary and religious life. The Law could never save anyone; it was a *taskmaster* (Galatians 3:24) which brought man to the full realization that no one could live as righteous as God demanded, and sin resulted in death and condemnation. The Law was good but it was flawed. It condemned man kind and could never save anyone from eternal condemnation.

Dispensation of Grace

The New Covenant ushered in a new period of time called the *Dispensation of Grace*. The Dispensation of Grace is still in effect today, and will continue until the 2nd advent of Christ. Our Lord and Savior Jesus Christ came not to destroy the Law but to fulfill the law. His sacrificial death as the perfect Lamb of God on the Cross of Calvary ended the Dispensation of the Law. Redemption from sin… salvation… and the gift of eternal life… was now based upon *faith* and appropriated by grace. Salvation by faith and grace began what we now call the *New Covenant*. When Jesus Christ died on the Cross of calvary, He was the perfect and final sacrifice for the forgiveness of sin. All Old Testament sacrifices were simply an atonement or a covering for sin. Both Old Testament sins and sins before the law came were paid for by Christ as He died on the Cross. Salvation and forgiveness of sins… past, present and future were settled forever.

The Dispensation of Grace started in 30 AD and will continue until Jesus Christ returns as a conquering king at His 2nd advent. The 2nd advent of Christ is generally identified as taking place on the Jewish *Feast of Yom Kippur*. Note that this belief does not predict the time and date of the 2nd advent of Christ. It does not even predict the day of the week since the Feast of Yom Kippur can fall on a different day in different years.

A study of the Seven Feasts of Israel is highly recommended for anyone who wants to understand the 1st and 2nd coming of our Lord Jesus Christ. The 1st 4 feasts of Israel are all held in the Spring, and each is to remember how God saved Israel from Egyptian servitude and slavery…and they are still observed today by all Jews. The 7 Feasts of Israel are not only to honor God and remember the Exodus, but they are also called *Moeds* which means a *rehearsal*. Rehearsal for what? Every one of the 4 Spring feasts were a rehearsal for the coming of Jesus Christ and each were satisfied completely by His 1st advent. It is widely accepted and believed that the last 3 Feasts of Israel…which are held in the same month every Spring…. will be completely satisfied and realized by Jesus Christ in His 2nd advent. The interested reader is encouraged to study: Phillips, The Book of Revelation; *Mysteries Revealed*.

The Millennial Dispensation

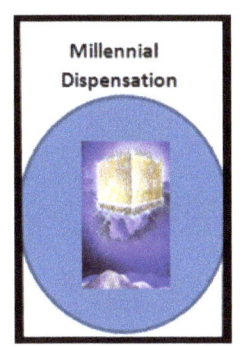

The seventh and final *Millennial Dispensation* will begin after the great Tribulation ends and the *Battle of Armageddon* is fought at the end of the Church Age. The 1000-year *Millennial Kingdom* will begin after the *Battle of Armageddon* is fought outside of Jerusalem; after the *Bema Seat Judgment* of all believers for rewards; and after the *Judgment of the Nations* (See Chapter 4). The Millennial Dispensation will last 1,000 years and is commonly referred to as the *Millennial Kingdom*. The word *Millennial* never appears in scripture, but has been constructed from two Latin words; *Mille* which means *thousand* and *annul* which means *year*. The beginning of the Millennial Kingdom will initiate a 1000 period of time during which Jesus Christ will rule and reign *on this earth* from His palace and throne in *Jerusalem*. His Kingdom will be worldwide but it will begin with a Jewish remnant from each of the 12 tribes of Israel who will finally inherit and live on the land that God promised to Abraham long ago. The 1,000-year Millennial Kingdom will end in a new heaven and a new earth (Revelation 21:1). This earth as we now know it will be purged by fire and restored to an Edenic state: Eternity will then begin.

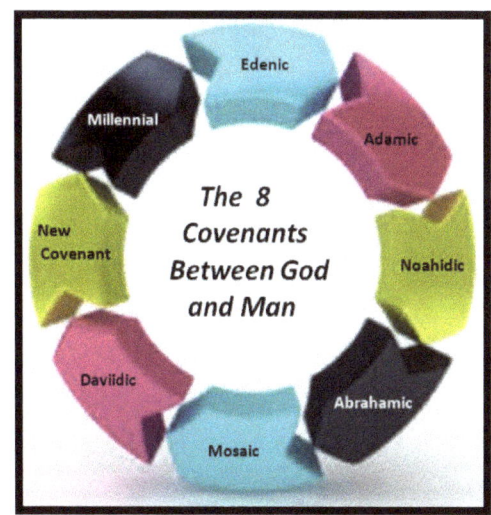

It is impossible to understand the Millennial Kingdom without understanding its purpose in God's plan for both the people and the earth that He has created. *The Church* Age and the *Great Tribulation* will come to an end. Before the

Millennial Kingdom will begin, every saint will have been raised from the grave or *raptured* out of an evil world. After the *Wrath of God* is poured out on a sinful world (the 7 Bowl /Vial) Judgments (Revelation 15:1, Revelation 16:1), Satan and his army will be defeated at the Battle of Armageddon: The Antichrist and the False Prophet will be cast into the *Lake of Burning Fire*, and Satan will be bound and cast into the *Bottomless Pit*. After the Battle of Armageddon, the Bema Seat Judgment for reward of all the saints and the Judgment of the Nations will then be held.

The Covenants of God

There are 8 major covenants which God has made with man. These covenants are spread over the 7 different dispensations already briefly discussed. These seven *Dispensations* divide the full council of God's word and His plan for mankind into seven distinct periods of time. Each Dispensation starts  with a distinct event after which God will deal with man in a particularly different way. Equally important is the concept of a *Covenant Relationship* between God and mankind. A **covenant is a sacred agreement between God and a person or a set of people.** The Greek word for covenant can also mean *promise*. A *covenant* is not the same as a *rule* or a *law*. A covenant as we use the term is an agreement between God and either an individual or a group of individuals. Covenants are always based upon one or more conditions or laws, but the conditions and laws associated with a covenant are agreements or commands upon which a covenant (promise) is based upon.

When God makes a covenant promise with mankind, there are always specific conditions and agreements between the two parties. Man's relationship to God has always been largely based upon covenantal promises. The study of *Biblical Covenants* is central to understanding how God has dealt with man and the sin issue throughout the seven dispensations. Different dispensations always operate under specific covenant relationships with God, but not all dispensations are defined by covenants. Specific covenants between God and man can start and end *anywhere* across the spectrum of the seven dispensations and usually exist through more than one dispensation. Understanding the way covenants operate within and between the seven different dispensations will reveal to man how to *rightly divide the word of God.* Covenants between God and man fall into two mutually exclusive and independent categories. They are either (1) *Conditional,* or (2) *Unconditional.*

Conditional Covenants

A *conditional covenant* usually depends on the faithfulness of one or more parties, and the covenant is invalidated if either party should break the conditions of the covenant. Whenever a conditional covenant is made between God and man, if the covenant promises are made null and void, the trespass is *always* by man and not by God. This is sometimes misunderstood: God will never invalidate or change the conditions of an *unconditional covenant* made by Him, but He is justified in annulling a *conditional* covenant if man fails to keep the conditions of the covenant. The classic example of a conditional covenant between God and man was the one that God made to Adam and Eve in the Garden of Eden. The Lord made the Garden of Eden for Adam and Eve to live in forever. He gave them dominion over all of the creatures that He had made, and provided for everything that they might need. They were to commune with God and live forever by eating of the Tree of Life. God *promised* Adam and Eve that this would go on forever. This covenant with Adam and Eve depended upon only *one Law* that could not be broken.

But of the tree of the knowledge of good and evil, thou shalt not eat of it: for in the day that thou eat thereof thou shalt surely die   Genesis 2:17

Adam and Eve violated their covenant with God and ate of the *tree of the knowledge of good and evil* which rendered their covenant with God null and void.

Another example of a conditional covenant between God and man took place at Mt. Sinai after the exodus from Egypt. When Israel reached Mount Sinai 47 days after leaving Egypt, Moses went up on the mountain and met with God.

[3] And Moses went up unto God, and the LORD called unto him out of the mountain, saying, Thus shalt thou say to the house of Jacob, and tell the children of Israel;
[4] Ye have seen what I did unto the Egyptians, and how I bare you on eagles' wings, and brought you unto myself.

[5] *Now therefore, **if ye will obey my voice** indeed, and **keep my covenant**, then ye shall be a **peculiar treasure** unto me above all people: for all the earth is mine:*
[6] And ye shall be unto me a kingdom of priests, and an holy nation. These are the words which thou shalt speak unto the children of Israel
[8] And all the people answered together, and said: All that the LORD hath spoken we will do   Exodus 19: 3-6

Sadly, within days the people were worshipping idols of gold. They soon lost their *treasure* by getting worse and worse. Finally, God had all 12 tribes taken into captivity by Assyria and then Babylon, and the City of Jerusalem was burned and ransacked. This is why their land of promise is still largely in foreign hands today.

Unconditional Covenants

An *unconditional covenant* is one that is not dependent on the faithfulness of either party, but remains valid from its point of initiation until it is fulfilled. Unconditional covenants are unilateral between God and man. The interesting thing about an unconditional covenant between God and man is that no matter how unfaithful or disobedient man might be, the covenant (promise) will always be fulfilled because God is faithful and true and cannot lie. What God promises unconditionally, He will fulfill. We will see that unconditional covenants initiated by God to Abraham over 3500 years ago continue to be in effect from the moment that God stated His promises until the promises come true, no matter how much time might elapse. There may or may not be conditions to be met by man when God makes an unconditional covenant. Violation of any conditions may delay the fulfillment of the covenant, but will not cancel the promise(s) of God. Covenants in the Bible between God and man are always originated by God and are an act of His holiness and grace. Since God is faithful and true (Jeremiah 42:5), He cannot lie and cannot sin. *Conditional covenants* between God and man *always* terminate because of the unfaithfulness and the sinful nature of man. *Unconditional Covenants* between God and man may be delayed, but will always be fulfilled. There were eight main covenants made between God and man throughout Biblical history.

- **The Edenic Covenant**
- **The Adamic Covenant**
- **The Noahidic Covenant**
- **The Abrahamic Covenant**
- **The Mosaic or Old Covenant**
- **The Davidic Covenant**

- **The Covenant of Grace or the New Covenant**
- **The Millennial or Kingdom Covenant**

The diagram on the next page illustrates the timing and relationship between each of the seven different dispensations and the eight covenants which were made between God and man. The key event which triggers each dispensation is also given, along with the approximate date that each of the seven dispensations begin and end. Except for the *Davidic Covenant*, the year in which each covenant is given corresponds to a dispensation start date. However, the duration of each covenant might span one or more dispensations...... particularly if the covenant is unconditional.

The Eight Covenants Between God and Man

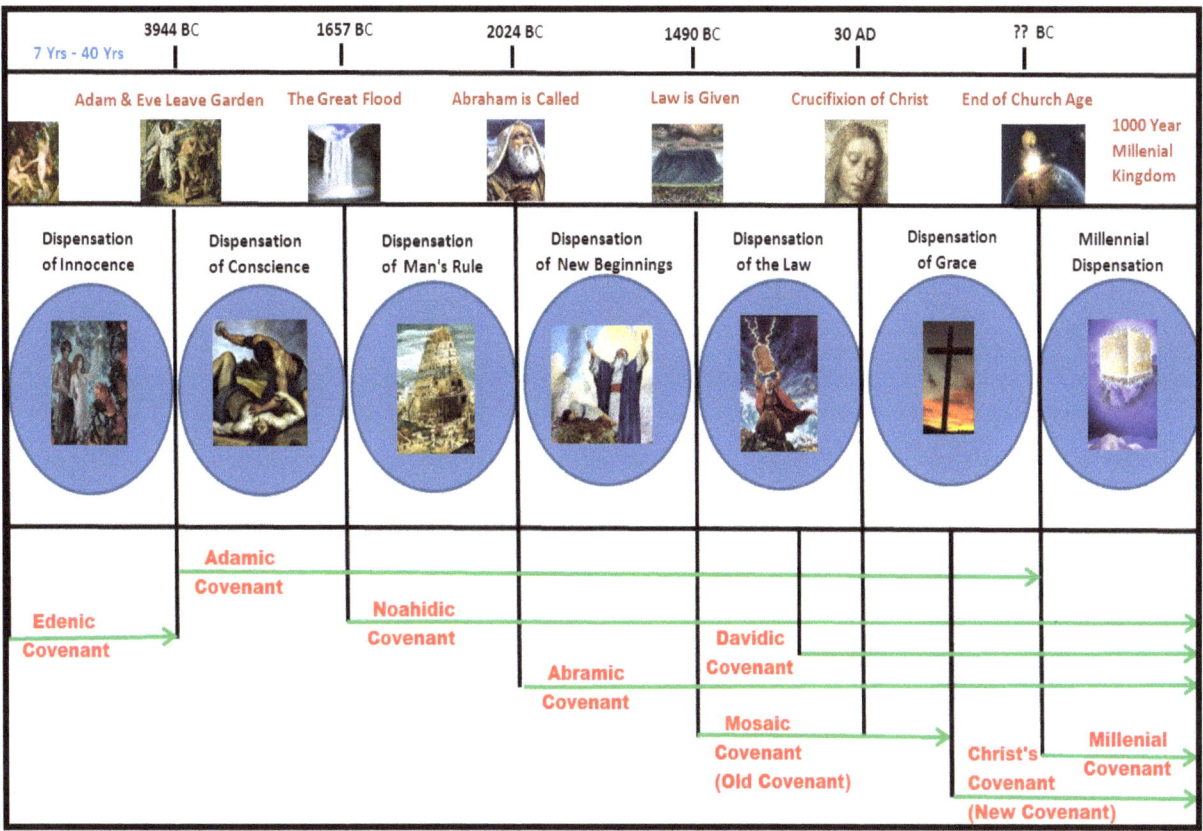

The Edenic Covenant (Genesis 1-3)

The Edenic Covenant was between God, Adam and Eve, and included the command to multiply and to populate the earth with their offspring. The Edenic Covenant also promised dominion over the earth and life everlasting in return for obedience. However, the most important restriction was to never eat from the tree of the knowledge of good and evil. This *covenant* contained a terrible penalty for disobedience; if violated, both Adam and Eve would *surely die*.

Adamic Covenant (Genesis 1:26-30, 2:16-17)
As a result of Adam and Eve breaking the Edenic Covenant, enmity was established between Satan and the descendants of Adam. From the moment that Eve sinned and was expunged from the Garden of Eden, all women would experience pain in childbirth. The soil was cursed and thorns and thistles would grow in the earth. Man would no longer be sustained by food from the trees which grew in the Garden, but the earth would need to be planted, cultivated and harvested by the sweat and toil of man. Finally, every man or woman would experience death.

Noahidic Covenant (Genesis 9:11)
The first use of the word covenant in the scriptures occurs in Genesis 6:18. The actual covenant is given in Genesis 9:11. The Noahidic Covenant was spoken to Noah following the departure of Noah, his family, and all of the animals from the ark:

> *I* (will) *establish my covenant with you, that never again shall all flesh be cut off by the waters of the flood, and never again shall there be a flood to destroy the earth*   Genesis 9:11

This covenant included a sign of God's faithfulness to keep His word; a rainbow would appear in the sky when it rained. This covenant was *unconditional* and did not depend upon the faithfulness of either Noah or his descendants.

Abrahamic Covenant. (Genesis 15, II Samuel 11:7-16,
II Chronicles 17:10-14)
This *covenant*, first made to Abraham in Genesis 12: 1-3 was reinforced and expanded across Genesis 12 to Genesis 22. It was an extensive and far-reaching covenant between Abram (Abraham) and all of his offspring. We will not discuss this in great detail, but it contained *four* fundamental promises: (1) God pronounced a blessing upon Abram, to make his name great and to make his seed into a great nation, (2) The covenant promised that Abram's blessing would be extended to many people and nations. A blessing would fall upon all those who blessed Abraham and a curse would fall upon those who cursed him, (3) God vowed to bless the entire world through Abram's seed; the fulfillment of this part of the covenant is through Jesus Christ, who was of Abraham's family line, through

Sarah, Isaac, Jacob and Leah from which Judah was born and eventually Jesus Christ (4) The fourth basic covenant was that Abram's seed would be given what is now called the *Land of Canaan* as a *perpetual inheritance*. When God finished declaring all of the promises of His covenant with Abram, He caused him to fall into a deep sleep. He then took some animals and birds, killed them, placed them in a parallel path, sprinkled their blood over the path and then passed between the animals. This was a *blood oath* in which He swore by Himself (unilaterally) that all of His promises would be fulfilled. He then changed the name of Abram to Abraham to ratify the covenant. This was an *unconditional covenant* known as the *Abramic Covenant*. Later, God gave Abraham the rite of *circumcision* as the specific sign of the Abrahamic Covenant (Genesis 17:9–14). It is important that one part of this unconditional covenant with Abraham was a *land covenant*. The Abrahamic Covenant included the promise of land which they would one day inhabit (Genesis 12:1). It was a specific piece of land called the Promised Land or the Land of Milk and Honey. The boundaries included all of the land between the Euphrates River to the north, the Egyptian River to the south, the Mediterranean Sea to the West and the Dead Sea to the East. The unconditional promise was later clearly specified to include a portion of the land for each of 12 tribes of Israel. We will see that this promise is fundamental to understanding why the Millennial Kingdom has to be a 1000-year period of time during which 12 tribes of Israel will live in peace and prosperity on the land which was promised to Abraham, and later reiterated in promises to Moses and King David. The Abrahamic Covenant was repeated in Deuteronomy 30: 1–10 and to Joshua and the 12 tribes of Israel before they crossed the River Jordan..

It must be recognized that when Israel crossed the River Jordan after the 40 year exodus from Egypt, Israel did conquer and live upon a portion of this land called the *Land of Canaan*. But they apostatized, did not trust God to vanquish all of their enemies in conquering the land, and failed to conquer *all* the land promised to them at that time. Israel has *never* inherited all of the land promised to Abraham, Moses and King David.... but they will. This is the main purpose of the Millennial Kingdom and it will come to pass. The portions of land assigned to each tribe and the dimensions of each piece are given in Ezekiel 40-45. Even though Israel apostatized and violated their part of the covenant, God is not going to renege on His promise. Centuries after Abraham died, the children of Israel took possession of most of the land under Joshua's leadership (Joshua 21:43). However, at no point in history has Israel controlled all of the land God had promised to them. There remains, therefore, a final fulfillment of the *Abrahamic Covenant* that will see Israel occupying their God-given homeland to the fullest extent. The fulfillment will be more than a matter of geography; it will also be a time of holiness and restoration (Ezekiel 20: 40–44 and Ezekiel 36:1—37:28).

Mosaic Covenant (Exodus 20-Deuteronomy 28)

The *Mosaic Covenant* is sometimes called the *Old Covenant*. This covenant is found scattered between Exodus 20 and Deuteronomy 28. It promised the Israelites a blessing for obedience and a curse for disobedience. Much of the Old Testament chronicles the fulfillment of cycles of judgment for sin and blessings when God's people lost faith, repented and returned to God. The Mosaic Covenant is sometimes called the *Sinai Covenant* because it was first spoken at Mount Sinai after Israel had been saved from death by the pursuing Pharaoh and his army by the waters of the Red Sea. The Mosaic Covenant was a *conditional covenant* between God and Israel. God made a covenant with Israel that if they would obey His laws and separate themselves from the Gentile world that He would bless and protect them (Exodus 19: 5-8). The Mosaic covenant was different from the Abramic Covenant: The Mosaic covenant was *conditional* and depended upon whether or not the Nation of Israel would obey God. The Abramic covenant was unconditional. The blessings and fulfillment of God's promises under the Mosaic (Old) covenant rested upon how Israel would respond to the commands of God. There were basically 3 Covenant promises made to Israel by God.

1.0 The Jews would be God's chosen people and He would bless them above all other nations.
2.0 The nation of Israel would be a Kingdom of Priests
3.0 Israel would be a holy nation
4.0 Any nation or people that would bless Israel would be blessed, and any nation that would curse Israel would be cursed
 Exodus 19: 3-6

When God made His covenant with Israel at Mount Sinai the people all loudly proclaimed: *All that the Lord has spoken we will do* (Exodus 19:8).

Davidic Covenant (II Samuel 7:8-16).

The *Davidic Covenant* is actually a reassurance and expansion of the Abrahamic and the Mosaic Covenant. This *unconditional covenant* was given to King David, and reinforced the land Covenant given to Abraham and his seed. This is sometimes called the *Palestinian Covenant*. Neither is quite correct since the Davidic Covenant involved more than just the land of Palestine, and the original land Covenant which was given to Abraham was much larger than the land which was conquered and settled by Israel after Joshua crossed the Jordan River. Inherent in the covenant promise of God was that if Israel would not obey Him and follow His laws, God would allow other nations to conquer Israel and carry them into captivity.

When King Solomon died, his United Kingdom was ripped into two parts: One was the Northern Kingdom (Israel) and the other was the Southern Kingdom (Judah). After about 200 years, the Northern Kingdom was completely conquered and taken into captivity by Assyria. Only 200 years later, the Southern Kingdom was conquered and taken into captivity for 70 years by Nebuchadnezzar and the Babylonian Empire. Ten of the 12 tribes of Israel from the Northern Kingdom had been previously taken into captivity by the Assyrians and were never heard from again. We call these the *Lost 10 tribes of Israel*.

All 12 tribes *will* be united again and eventually be restored to *all* the land of promise in the Millennial Kingdom. This covenant will not be fulfilled until after the *fullness of the Gentiles* has been completed.

For I would not, brethren, that ye should be ignorant of this mystery, lest ye should be wise in your own conceits; that blindness in part is happened to Israel, until the fullness of the Gentiles be come in   Romans 11:25

After the *fullness of the Gentiles has come in*, the Jews as a nation will turn to Jesus Christ as their promised Messiah. This will happen at the end of the great tribulation period described by the Apostle John in the Book of Revelation.

And so all Israel shall be saved: as it is written, There shall come out of Zion the Deliverer, and shall turn away ungodliness from Jacob   Romans 11:26

        Covenant of Grace (Jeremiah 31: 31-34, Matthew 26:28)
The Covenant of Grace is often called the *New Covenant*. This covenant was ratified by Jesus Christ, the Son of God, at the Lord's Last Supper (Luke 22:20). Within 12 hours He would be sacrificed on the cross of Calvary and through His sacrificial death He would take away the sins of the whole world (I John 2:2). The death of Christ confirmed the unilateral covenant promise that God made to Adam after Adam and Eve were cast out of the Garden of Eden (Genesis 3:15), and it fulfilled the words of Jeremiah (Jeremiah 31:31-34) and many other Old Testament prophets. That covenant was that a Messiah would be sent from God to permanently forgive sins and save the people. Justification and propitiation of sin

for *all* people was settled on the cross. However, there was a conditional covenant made with all people that did not involve sin but faith. Forgiveness of sins was accomplished on the cross, but that only opened the path to salvation. Eternal life can never be obtained without *faith*.... Faith that Jesus Christ is the only Son of God who came to forgive all sins and that He will one day return and resurrect all who would believe from death and the grave. Eternal life is a free Gift of God by grace but it can only be appropriated by *Faith*.

Millennial Covenant

The *Millennial Covenant* is sometimes called the *Kingdom Covenant*. The Millennial covenant was spoken of and prophesied by prophets of God that arose throughout all of scripture. The Millennial Kingdom was repeatedly alluded to by Jesus Christ during His earthly ministry. The phrase Millennial Kingdom does not appear anywhere in scripture, but it corresponds to the 1,000-year dispensation that will immediately follow the Tribulation Period described in the Book of Revelation. We discuss the Millennial Kingdom promises in detail because of its significance in God's eternal plan for mankind. The most definitive revelation of the Millennial Kingdom to come is found in the book of Revelation.

[1] *And I saw an angel come down from heaven, having the key of the bottomless pit and a great chain in his hand.*
[2] *And he laid hold on the dragon, that old serpent, which is the Devil, and Satan, and bound him* **a thousand years**,
[3] *And cast him into the bottomless pit, and shut him up, and set a seal upon him, that he should deceive the nations no more, till* **the thousand years** *should be fulfilled: and after that he must be loosed a little season.*
[4] *And I saw thrones, and they sat upon them, and judgment was given unto them: and I saw the souls of them that were beheaded for the witness of Jesus, and for the word of God, and which had not worshipped the beast, neither his image, neither had received his mark upon their foreheads, or in their hands; and they lived and reigned with Christ a thousand years.*
[5] *But the rest of the dead lived not again until* **the thousand years** *were finished. This is the first resurrection.*
[6] *Blessed and holy is he that hath part in the first resurrection: on such the second death hath no power, but they shall be priests of God and of Christ, and shall reign with him* **a thousand years.**
[7] *And when* **the thousand years** *are expired, Satan shall be loosed out of his prison,*

[8] And shall go out to deceive the nations which are in the four quarters of the earth, Gog and Magog, to gather them together to battle: the number of whom is as the sand of the sea.
[9] And they went up on the breadth of the earth, and compassed the camp of the saints about, and the beloved city: and fire came down from God out of heaven, and devoured them.
[10] And the devil that deceived them was cast into the lake of fire and brimstone, where the beast and the false prophet are, and shall be tormented day and night forever and ever.
[11] And I saw a great white throne, and him that sat on it, from whose face the earth and the heaven fled away; and there was found no place for them.
[12] And I saw the dead, small and great, stand before God; and the books were opened: and another book was opened, which is the book of life: and the dead were judged out of those things which were written in the books, according to their works.
[13] And the sea gave up the dead which were in it; and death and hell delivered up the dead which were in them: and they were judged every man according to their works.
[14] And death and hell were cast into the lake of fire. This is the second death.
[15] And whosoever was not found written in the book of life was cast into the lake of fire.   Revelation 20: 1-15

Promise of the Land

One of the most important and far-reaching events in the history of Israel was the Abramic Covenant made with Abraham when he was living in Ur of the Chaldees. When God called him forth to father the Nation of Israel, He promised (Covenanted) with Abram that:

[2] I will make of thee a great nation, and I will bless thee, and make thy name great; and thou shalt be a blessing:
[3] And I will bless them that bless thee, and curse him that curseth thee: and in thee shall all families of the earth be blessed.
[4] So Abram departed, as the LORD had spoken unto him; and Lot went with him: and Abram was seventy and five years old when he departed out of Haran.
*[5] And Abram took Sarai his wife, and Lot his brother's son, and all their substance that they had gathered, and the souls that they had gotten in Haran; and they went forth to go into the **land of Canaan**; and into the land of Canaan they came.*

[6] And Abram passed through the land unto the place of Sichem, unto the plain of Moreh. And the Canaanite was then in the land.
[7] And the LORD appeared unto Abram, and said: **Unto thy seed will I give this land**   Genesis 12: 2-7

God at that time gave Abram and his seed all of the land that he could see.

[14] And the LORD said unto Abram, after that Lot was separated from him, Lift up now thine eyes, and look from the place where thou art northward, and southward, and eastward, and westward:
[15] For all the land which thou see, to thee will I give it, and to thy seed ***forever***
Genesis 13: 14-15

The extent of this land promise was later clarified and defined in Genesis 15 and in Deuteronomy 30.

In the same day the LORD made a covenant with Abram, saying: Unto thy seed have I given this land, from the river of Egypt unto the great river, the river Euphrates   Genesis 15:18

[3] That then the LORD thy God will turn thy captivity, and have compassion upon thee, and will return and gather thee from all the nations, whither the LORD thy God hath scattered thee.
[4] If any of thine be driven out unto the outmost parts of heaven, from thence will the LORD thy God gather thee, and from thence will he fetch thee
Deuteronomy 30: 3-4

God also promised the people of Israel that *He* would gather the dispersed people of Israel back into the land. This was not the return of Israel from 70 years of Babylonian Captivity and this is not the steady migration of the Jews back to Israel since Israel became a nation again on May 14, 1948. This is a prophecy concerning the return of all the 12 tribes of Israel to inherit and live in the land that God promised to them. Many television evangelists and well-meaning Christians have boldly declared that because the Jews are returning to Israel today that the tribulation period is about to begin. This cannot not be true because the tribulation period of time described by John in the Book of Revelation *must be completed* before the Millennial Kingdom can begin, God recovers a remnant of Jews back to

Israel, and the land is divided among 12 tribes of Israel. The return of many Jews to Israel since May 8, 1948 is *not* a fulfillment of Deuteronomy 30: 3-4.

The Lord *himself* will regather His chosen people into Israel *after* the Church Age has finished and not before. The regathering of Israel is mentioned in a multitude of bible prophecies. The Jews have been conquered by the Assyrians, the Babylonians and the Romans; and they experienced horrible and senseless genocide under the Germans in WW II. This is all because they failed to uphold the conditional Mosaic Covenant. In spite of their domination by the Gentiles they have never lost their identity and have clung to the Old Testament economy of salvation by works. What is taking place today is **not** the calling of Israel back to their promised land. Every Christian today who has been saved by grace and has had their sins forgiven by Jesus Christ on the Cross of Calvary should pray every day that The Jews will have the scales removed from their eyes that have temporarily blinded them in part. Then and only then will they accept Jesus Christ as their Lord and Savior.

[25] *For I would not, brethren, that ye should be ignorant of this mystery, lest ye should be wise in your own conceits; that blindness in part is happened to Israel, until the fullness of the Gentiles be come in.*
[26] *And so all Israel shall be saved: as it is written, There shall come out of Zion the Deliverer, and shall turn away ungodliness from Jacob*:
[27] *For this is my **covenant** unto them, when I shall take away their sins*
Romans 11:25-27

And so, it will come to pass that: All of Israel will be saved. Consider the following Old Testament prophecies.

[10] *And **in that day** there shall be **a root of Jesse**, which shall stand for an ensign of the people; to it shall the Gentiles seek: and his rest shall be glorious.*
[11] *And it shall come to pass **in that day**, that the Lord shall set his hand again the **second time to recover the remnant of his people**, which shall be left: From Assyria, and from Egypt, and from Pathros, and from Cush, and from Elam, and from Shinar, and from Hamath, and from the islands of the sea.*
[12] *And he shall set up an **ensign for the nations**, and shall assemble the outcasts*

*of Israel, and **gather together the dispersed of Judah from the four corners of the earth***   Isaiah 11: 10-12

The *Day of the Lord* of which Isaiah prophesied was identified previously in Isaiah 2 and the *Root of Jessie* is Jesus Christ. A *remnant* will be regathered to the promised Land from the *four corners of the earth. And it shall come to pass in that day, that the Lord shall set his hand again the **second** time to recover the remnant of his people* (Isaiah 11:11). The 1st time was after the 70-year Babylonian captivity.

[21] *And say unto them, Thus saith the Lord GOD; Behold, I will take the children of Israel from among the heathen, where they be gone, and will gather them on every side, and **bring them into their own land:***
[22] *And I will make them **one nation** in the land upon the mountains of Israel; and **one king** shall be king to them all: and they shall be no more two nations, neither shall they be divided into two kingdoms any more at all:*
[23] *Neither shall they defile themselves any more with their idols, nor with their detestable things, nor with any of their transgressions: but I will save them out of all their dwelling places, wherein they have sinned, and will **cleanse them**: so shall they be my people, and I will be their God.*
[24] *And **David my servant shall be king over them**; and they all shall have one shepherd: they shall also walk in my judgments, and observe my statutes, and do them.*
[25] ***And they shall dwell in the land that I have given unto Jacob** my servant, wherein your fathers have dwelt; and they shall dwell therein, even they, and their children, and their children's children for ever: and my servant David shall be their prince **forever***   Ezekiel 37: 21-25

Christ himself will supernaturally gather those Jews that are alive and remain to inhabit the 1000-year millennial Kingdom after the Tribulation Period has ended at the Battle of Armageddon. This cannot be referring to the gathering of the people to Moses at the Exodus because Isaiah promised that a *remnant* would be regathered the second time from each of 12 tribes of Israel.: *For though thy people Israel be as the sand of the sea, yet a **remnant** of them shall return* (Isaiah 10:22) Ezekiel 37: 21-25 cannot refer to either the return from Babylonian exile or the exodus from Egypt. At the exodus from Egypt *all of the people* left Egypt with Moses at that time. When the Jews were regathered to Israel and Jerusalem after the 70 years of Babylonian captivity, only 2 1/2 tribes from the Southern Kingdom returned. In addition, when Israel is regathered by God to populate the Millennial Kingdom Jerusalem and the surrounding area will be leveled by a great earthquake.... The area which now holds the temple mount will be raised up to a large plateau.... and the *Throne of Jesus Christ* will be built from which He will rule and reign over all nations. King David will be resurrected and reign beside Christ over all Israel. This was prophesied by the prophet Ezekiel.

[21] *And say unto them, Thus saith the Lord GOD; Behold, I will take the children of Israel from among the heathen, where they be gone, and will gather them on every side, and bring them into their own land:*
[22] *And I will make them one nation in the land upon the mountains of Israel; and one king shall be king to them all: and they shall be no more two nations, neither shall they be divided into two kingdoms any more at all:*
[23] *Neither shall they defile themselves any more with their idols, nor with their detestable things, nor with any of their transgressions: but I will save them out of all their dwelling places, wherein they have sinned, and will cleanse them: so shall they be my people, and I will be their God.*
[24] *And David my servant shall be king over them; and they all shall have one shepherd: they shall also walk in my judgments, and observe my statutes, and do them.*
[25] *And they shall dwell in the land that I have given unto Jacob my servant, wherein your fathers have dwelt; and they shall dwell therein, even they, and their children, and their children's children for ever: and my servant David shall be their prince forever*   Ezekiel 37:24

The Lord will rule over the whole world from a mountain that will be raised above the land surrounding Jerusalem (See Phillips: *Life After the Great Tribulation*).

[2] *And it shall come to pass in the last days,* **that** *the mountain of the LORD's house shall be established in the top of the mountains, and shall be exalted above the hills; and all nations shall flow unto it.*
[11] The *lofty looks of man shall be humbled, and the haughtiness of men shall be bowed down, and the LORD alone shall be exalted in* **that** *day.*

[12] For *the day of the LORD of hosts shall be upon every one **that** is proud and lofty, and upon every one **that** is lifted up; and he shall be brought low:*
[17] And *the loftiness of man shall be bowed down, and the haughtiness of men shall be made low: and the LORD alone shall be exalted in **that** day.*
[20] In *that day a man shall cast his idols of silver, and his idols of gold, which they made each one for himself to worship, to the moles and to the bats*
Isaiah 2: 2, 11-12, 17, 20

The *Mountain of the Lord's House* is where Jesus Christ will rule and reign during the Millennial Kingdom. *ALL* nations will worship there. The god of the Muslims and gods of the Hindus will no longer be worshipped…only Jesus Christ here on earth, and Jehovah God in His heavenly home. This can only happen when Christ rules in the Millennial Kingdom.

There are many other places in the Old Testament that testify Israel is destined to inherit **all** of the land that was promised to them by the Abramic and Davidic covenants; God will regather all of His chosen people that remain alive from the four corners of the world; and Jesus Christ with King David will rule and reign *on this earth* during the 1000-year Millennial Kingdom.

We are now ready to describe 21 different occasions when God executed righteous judgment upon those who willingly and purposely refused to follow the commands of God. There are 3 future judgments of God which will take place between the 2nd coming of Christ and the Battle of Armageddon…and the Millennial Kingdom. One final judgment will be described which will take place after the 1000-year Millennial Kingdom has run its course.

Chapter 2

Judgment and The Wrath of God

Many Christians do not want to discuss or even understand the judgment and subsequent Wrath of God. The premise is that God is love (I John 4:16, Deuteronomy 7:9), and if God is the very substance and essence of love, He cannot be a God of Wrath. This theology is not consistent with what is taught in the Word of God. It is this very belief that cause so many Christians to believe that no Christian will ever go through the Great Tribulation period which will result in the end of the age. A popular belief is that every Christian should just "hang on" until one day every living Christian will be *caught up* or *raptured out* of this evil world in a pre-tribulation rapture of all living ecclesia or true believers at that time. Nothing could be farther from the truth (Phillips, *Rapture and Resurrection*). A blood-bought Christian is assured of eternal life in Jesus Christ by the redeeming work of Jesus Christ on the Cross of Calvary, but no true believer in Jesus Christ was ever promised that they would escape tribulation in this world, only that they would escape the Wrath of God which are the 7 Bowl Judgments of God (Revelation 15:1, Revelation 16:1).

Know therefore that the LORD thy God, he is God, the faithful God, which keep covenant and mercy with them that love him and keep his commandments to a thousand generations   Deuteronomy 7:9

These things I have spoken unto you, that in me ye might have peace. ***In the world ye shall have tribulation****: but be of good cheer; I have overcome the world*
John 16:33

Rejoicing in hope; patient in ***tribulation****; continuing instant in prayer*   Romans 12:12

This book is concerned with how God has already judged man or will judge man in the future. These are judgments and Wrath of God justified by the actions of man. The judgments described in the Old Testament often resulted in *physical* death. There are three judgments which will be described in Chapter 4 which can result in *spiritual death*. Judgment by God is part of who He is. The word *judgment* inherently contains the activity to *judge* either individuals or groups of individuals for disobeying his laws and commands. It can be difficult to read about God's judgment, especially in the Old Testament. Old Testament Judgment was always caused by sin, and almost always resulted in the execution of God's Wrath: Which sometimes even involved physical punishment, plagues, and sickness. God is holy and we are not. God, in His sovereignty, has a right to execute judgment any time he chooses, based on the fact that we are wicked, evil, sinful creatures. God's righteous judgment followed by Wrath was manifested in two ways: (1) *Individual judgment* and *wrath* or (2) *corporate judgment* and *wrath*. This is not a biblical distinction but one that is used in this book to at least partially define the scope of His punitive actions against sin. An example of individual judgment was God's judgment upon Moses when the children of Israel grumbled because they had no water (Numbers 20: 1-13). God instructed Moses to *speak to a rock* and He would provide water. Moses approached the rock and *struck it* twice with His rod. For this act of disobedience, Moses was not allowed to enter into the promised land. An example of a corporate judgment is the great flood. Every inhabitant of the earth had become sinful and wicked except for Noah, his three sons and all their wives. God had endured enough, and he destroyed (drowned) all but 8 people.

The great dividing line of God executing Judgment and Wrath upon man is the sacrificial death of Jesus Christ upon the Cross of Calvary. There is no record of God himself causing wrath to fall upon man in the New Testament except through the 7 Bowl judgments in the Book of Revelation (Revelation 15:1, Revelation 16:1). There are two incidents in the book of Acts which deserve mention. The first was in Acts 5: 1-11 in which Peter brought death upon both Ananias, and his wife Sapphira. The second was in Acts 13: 8-12) when Saul (Paul) caused Elymas the sorcerer to go blind.

There are two deaths which are clearly defined by God; (1) *Physical* death and (2) *Spiritual* death. Physical death is when we die and our lifeless body is placed in the grave. Spiritual death is eternal separation from God. Man is a living entity composed of 3 parts...*Body*, *Soul* and *Spirit*. When one dies, the body decays and returns to dust from which it came. The soul is taken to Paradise (Luke 23:43, II Corinthians 12:4), and the spirit returns to God from which it came (Phillips *Life After Death*, Ecclesiastes 12:7). God executed righteous judgment in the Old Testament upon people who were here on earth, but when death resulted it was physical death: This is called the *1st death*. The *2nd death* is spiritual death which is eternal separation from God (Revelation 21: 12-15). The opposite of holy is sin, and the opposite of life is death. Christ freed both Jew and Gentile of spiritual death when He died for all sins… past and present… on the Cross of Calvary.

The Old Testament is divided into two distinct parts. The 1st part consists of the first 4 dispensations and the 2nd part consists of the 5th dispensation. The great dividing line between the first 4 dispensations and the 5th dispensation is the *Law* which was given to Moses and His chosen people the Jews. Before the Law was given, God directly revealed His righteousness and commands to His people.

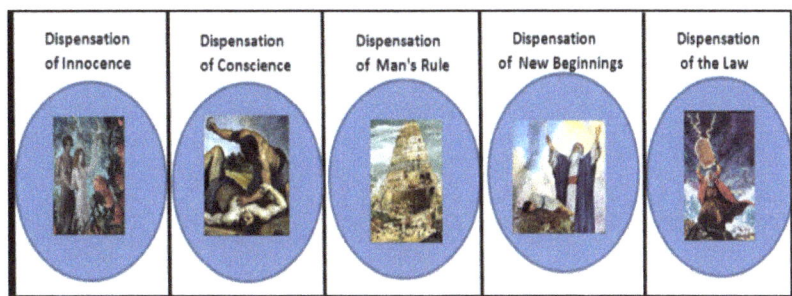

The Cross of Calvary and the sacrificial death of Christ is what separates the written Law and the Old Covenant from the last two dispensations of time.

  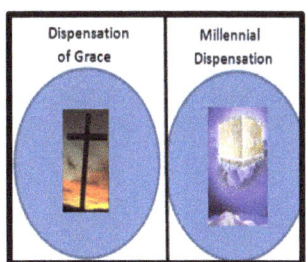

The *Dispensation of Innocence* was originally intended to last forever. God created man to walk and talk with Him in a sinless world. Man was created with an eternal soul and a mortal body which was intended to live forever. His earthly body would be sustained forever by the Tree of Life which grew in the Garden of Eden. The form of government by which God ruled is called a *theocracy*. A theocracy is a system of rule in which authority is exercised directly by God's sovereign rule over man. During this period of time there was no written law. There was also no knowledge of good and evil. There was only one command which God told Adam and Eve that they had to follow… they were not to eat of the *tree of knowledge of good and evil*. We all know the story… Satan tempted Eve and she ate of the forbidden fruit, and then so did Adam. This was the first sin, and because of their disobedience they could no longer eat of the Tree of Life which grew in the Garden of Eden. When both committed the 1st sin, they were expunged from the Garden and began to die (Genesis 2: 16-17). This was the first time that man caused God to change the way in which He would rule over man but it would not be the last. Man, and his evil sin nature, continually rebelled against God and interrupted his plans for the restoration of all things. The Dispensation of Innocence would be followed by the Dispensation of Conscience, The Dispensation of Man's rule and the Dispensation of New Beginnings. These three dispensations were characterized by God ruling as a theocracy and there was no written law.

There was a major change in the way that God would rule over man which took place when the Disposition of New beginnings ended and the Dispensation of Law began. When the law was given to Israel through Moses at Mt. Sinai (Exodus 19-Exodus 24), the 10 commandments were given to Israel by God and written on tablets of stone. God's chosen people were under the Law after Mt. Sinai, but God would still rule under a theocracy. He would visit with Moses in the tent of the meeting and instruct Moses on how to protect and lead his chosen people. Moses delivered the words of God and received miracles sent by God. God made a bilateral covenant with His chosen people.

At that time the *Mosaic Covenant* was initiated between God and the Nation of Israel. This covenant would set the nation of Israel apart from all other nations as God's chosen people. It was different from all other covenants which preceded it in that it was a *conditional covenant*. The Mosaic Covenant promised to make Israel and the Jews his own treasured possession, a holy, *unique and peculiar* people, set apart from all other nations. If Israel was obedient and followed the commands and laws of God, then God would bless them, but if they disobeyed, then God would punish them. The Mosaic Covenant was a conditional covenant which strengthened the promises to Abraham and his seed (plural) which was not conditional but unilateral. This was called the *Abramic Covenant* (Phillips, *The Eternal Plan of God*). The Mosaic Covenant is usually referred to as the *Old Covenant*.

Under the Old Covenant, there were only two types of people in the world: Jews and Gentiles. Gentiles were not a part of God's chosen people and in fact were considered to be heathens or *strangers at the gate*. The designation of a Jew refers to anyone who is an adherent to the religion *Judaism*, or anyone who is a member of the Jewish ethnic group. Judaism refers to both the religion and the ethnicity, as it predates the modern distinction between the two concepts. This is similar to modern Christianity. An American is anyone who is a citizen of the United States of America. Baptist, Lutherans, Methodists, etc. are Christian ethnic groups. Israel today is a mixture of many different religions, but it is predominately identified with the Jewish religion.

[3] *And Moses went up unto God, and the LORD called unto him out of the mountain, saying, Thus shalt thou say to the house of Jacob, and tell the children of Israel;*
[4] *Ye have seen what I did unto the Egyptians, and how I bare you on eagles' wings, and brought you unto myself.*
[5] *Now therefore, if ye will obey my voice indeed, and keep my covenant, then ye shall be a peculiar treasure unto me above all people: for all the earth is mine:*
[6] *And ye shall be unto me a kingdom of priests, and an holy nation. These are the words which thou shalt speak unto the children of Israel.*
[7] *And Moses came and called for the elders of the people, and laid before their faces all these words which the LORD commanded him.*
[8] *And all the people answered together, and said: All that the LORD hath spoken we will do. And Moses returned the words of the people unto the LORD*
Exodus 19: 3-8

He (Yahweh) would be their God and they (Israel) will be his chosen people. He gave man 613 different *social* laws which would govern their social behavior and dietary habits. God intended to personally rule over His people. He would bless them, vanquish their enemies and give them a promised land to live in and prosper. Of course, sinful man once again failed God. Around 1020 BC the people wanted Judges to rule over them, and in an act of grace, God granted their wish. Starting with Othniel, judges ruled under God for about 410 years. When Samuel was serving as the last judge, the people again became rebellious and said: *We want a king to rule over us. Then we will be like all the other nations, with a king to lead us and to go out before us and fight our battles* (I Samuel 8: 4-22). After inquiring of God, Samuel chose *Saul* to be the first King of Israel. Never again would Israel and the Jews be ruled by God under a theocracy, but they would be ruled by man. Once again, the chosen people of God had turned against Him.

The Disposition of the Law had begun as a theocracy and ended as a kingdom of chosen people ruled by Kings. As usual, when man acts upon his own will the consequences are never good. When King Solomon died, his United Kingdom was ripped into two parts by his own two sons: the Northern Kingdom of Israel and the Southern Kingdom of Judah. We will see in Chapter 3 that this act of rebellion and greed against God's initial plan for His people resulted in God moving Assyria to defeat and take the Northern Kingdom into exile, and then allow Babylon to defeat the Southern Kingdom of Judah, take the Jews into Babylonian captivity for 70 years, destroy the City of Jerusalem and burn Solomon's Temple.

Three Different Types of Judgment

Physical death is not judgment, but something that all will experience (Hebrews 9:27). Jesus tasted physical death at His crucifixion, but He conquered death and made a public spectacle of Satan when after 3 days in the tomb he arose and then ascended to heaven. *But we see Jesus, who was made a little lower than the angels for the suffering of death, crowned with glory and honor; that he by the grace of God should taste death for every man* (Hebrews 2:9). Because atonement of sins was accomplished at the cross: *There is therefore now no condemnation to them which are in Christ Jesus, who walk not after the flesh, but after the Spirit.* (Romans 8:1). It was also at the cross that God pronounced judgment on an unbelieving world and on Satan. Just before his crucifixion, Jesus said: *Now is the judgment of this world: now shall the prince of this world be cast out* John 12:31.

The Holy Scriptures teach that there are actually three different types of judgments: (1) *Temporal Judgments* by God or his Son (2) *Eternal or permanent Judgments* by Jesus Christ and (3) *Self Judgment*. The difference in temporal judgment and permanent judgment is that temporal judgment relates to individuals or groups of individuals here upon this earth, whereas permanent judgment concerns anyone who refuses to yield to either The Father or the Son. An example of a temporal, corporate judgment is the Babylonian Exile of the Kingdom of Judah which lasted 70 years. An example of Eternal or permanent judgment is the *Great white Throne Judgment* of all unbelievers. These will be discussed later in

Chapter 4. *Self Judgment* is seldom taught or recognized, but Self Judgment is that judgment which is inflicted upon oneself for acts of sin. Under the New Covenant, it is manifested in Christians and is a result of the Holy Spirit speaking to each individual in disagreement concerning sinful or rebellious actions. Self Judgment will often produce thoughts and feelings of anxiety, anger, and depression. Self judgment is a realization that man is weak, infallible and is imperfect. The body is drawn to acts of sin because the sin nature has been inherited from Adam, who is the progenitor of the human race. Satan is constantly trying to influence man to follow the ways of the world and engage in sinful acts or thinking. There is a constant battle which rages within man between the Holy Spirit and Satan. This conflict is what brings about self judgment. Sinful man lead by the Holy Spirit can only overcome the self judgment and condemnation which constantly admonishes and counsels the soul of man to overcome sin and to repent. The non-believer has no contact with God or the Holy Spirit and will not experience self judgment because there is no standard of righteousness or a moral compass in an unbeliever. An unbeliever is like a ship without a rudder, constantly being buffered by the wind and driven to anything that seems to be pleasurable.

Under the New Covenant, all eternal or permanent judgment and condemnation has been given to Jesus Christ. Matthew 25: 31-33 clearly tells us that the Son of Man is the Judge presiding over the *Judgment of the Nations* or the *Sheep and Goats Judgment* which will take place after the Battle of Armageddon. John 5:22 tells us that the Father will not judge anyone: He has committed all judgment to His Son, Jesus Christ. Christ will be the presiding judge at both the *Bema Seat Judgment* of all believers and the *Great White Throne Judgment* of all unbelievers. Under the New Covenant, He and He alone is worthy to reward those who believe in Him and condemn those who do not. Christ said:

Jesus saith unto him, I am the way, the truth, and the life: no man cometh unto the Father, but by me. John 14:6

Transgression against God, his holiness and His commands always results in wrath falling upon an individual, either in the form of temporary or self judgment here upon this earth, or permanently. Every Christian has placed his/her faith in Jesus Christ as their Lord and Savior. We have been promised by Christ under the New

Covenant that all of our sins will be forgiven by the blood of Jesus Christ. When a Christian sins, it is not part of a "free path" to do anything that man wants to do, but if a Christian sins it will always result in grief, remorse and regret. One of the roles of the Holy Spirit which lives in each true believer is to convict one of sin. The old sin nature inherited from Adam will temp the body to sin, but remorse and grief will always accompany any sinful act. The apostle Paul knew this painful fact when he struggled with the war between sin and grace.

[18] For I know that in me (that is, in my flesh,) dwelleth no good thing: for to will is present with me; but how to perform that which is good I find not.
[19] For the good that I would I do not: but the evil which I would not, that I do.
[20] Now if I do that I would not, it is no more I that do it, but sin that dwelleth in me.
[21] I find then a law, that, when I would do good, evil is present with me.
[22] For I delight in the law of God after the inward man:
[23] But I see another law in my members, warring against the law of my mind, and bringing me into captivity to the law of sin which is in my members.
[24] O wretched man that I am! who shall deliver me from the body of this death?
Romans 7: 18-24

Romans 7:24 is a rhetorical question: Paul knew full well the only man that could deliver him from sin and death was his Lord and savior Jesus Christ. That same man…Jesus Christ….is still the only one who can deliver us from death. The scriptures are very clear on this conclusion.

For the wages of sin is death; but the gift of God is eternal life through Jesus Christ our Lord. Romans 6:23

Righteous Judgment and the Wrath of God

The *Merriam-Webster dictionary* defines wrath as: *strong vengeful anger or indignation; retributory punishment for an offense or a crime: divine chastisement.* The dichotomy between the Wrath of God in the Old Testament and the Wrath of God in the New Testament reaches a great dividing line at the

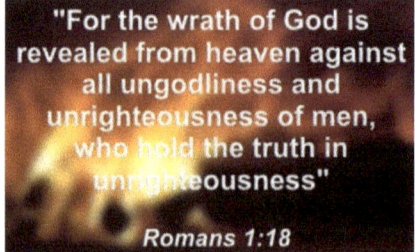

Cross of Calvary. The Old Testament is full of incidents where God executed temporal judgement upon mankind. He brought Wrath upon individuals, groups of individuals or large corporate groups of people. Chapter 3 will briefly discuss several of these judgments. Most Christians and pastors characterize God as only love and truth: Few teach or present God as equally being a God of Wrath. Many dichotomize God in the Old Testament as being a God of anger, vengeance and retribution; but one of love, mercy and longsuffering in the New Testament. This cannot be true if God is the same yesterday, today and tomorrow (Hebrews 13:8). This confusion can never be understood unless every New Covenant saint recognizes the dispensational divisions in the Holy bible. By definition, God dealt with His creation at different times in different ways. The holy trinity of God-Jesus Christ-Holy Spirit has always existed, although Jesus Christ was not manifested as the Son of God in the 1st five dispensations.

It will be observed that when God executed righteous judgment in the Old Testament, sentencing and wrath were by God alone. Some resulted in instant death and some as a curse which would be in effect until natural death. In all cases of instant death, this was the 1st death which is experienced by all men. By studying the New Testament, it is revealed that all judgment of mankind is reserved for the *Bema Seat Judgment* (judgment for rewards of all believers), the *Great White Throne Judgment* (judgment for eternal damnation of all unbelievers). The *Rod Judgment* by God in the wilderness (God's Judgment of the Jews) and the *Judgment of the Nations* (a combination of eternal damnation and rewards) … some will be condemned and some will be rewarded.

[**24**] *Verily, verily, I say unto you, He that heareth my word, and believeth on him that sent me, hath everlasting life, and shall not come into condemnation; but is passed from death unto life.*
[**25**] *Verily, verily, I say unto you,* **The hour is coming, and now is, when the dead shall hear the voice of the Son of God**: *and they that hear shall live.*
[**26**] *For as the Father hath life in himself; so hath he given to the Son to have life in himself;*
[**27**] **And hath given him authority to execute judgment** *also, because he is the Son of man.*
[**28**] *Marvel not at this: for the hour is coming, in the which **all** that are in the*

graves shall hear his voice,
[29] ***And shall come forth; they that have done good, unto the resurrection of life; and they that have done evil, unto the resurrection of damnation***
John 5: 24-29

And many of them that sleep in the dust of the earth shall awake, some to everlasting life, and some to shame and everlasting contempt   Daniel 12:2

... he (God) *hath appointed a day, in the which he* (Christ) *will judge the world in righteousness **by that man** whom he hath ordained; whereof he hath given assurance unto all men, in that he hath raised him from the dead*   Acts 17:31

God has given Jesus Christ the authority and power to execute final judgment and appointed him as the final tribunal. God has made His son Jesus Christ to be judge of all. This has divinely been decreed by the Father. The Greek word for "authority" is commonly translated as "power", and it implies all that is necessary to execute judgment: All the physical power to raise the dead, rule on the actions and thoughts of man; and to exercise the "moral right" or authority to sit in judgment on the creatures of God. The sentencing associated with eternal judgment is easy: Those who believed in faith upon Jesus Christ will be saved, and those who have rejected Jesus Christ as their Lord and savior have passed judgment upon themselves... They will experience the 2nd death and be eternally separated from God.

John...... and probably Luke in the Book of Acts...... both confirm that the Bema Seat Judgment, the Great White Throne Judgment and the Judgment of the Nations will all be final judgments which will be conducted by Jesus Christ. It is not clear exactly what role that God the Father will play in both the Bema Seat Judgment and the Great White Throne Judgment, but Jesus Christ has been given all power to reward all true believers and to sentence all unbelievers to the second death.

[11] *And I saw a great white throne, and him that sat on it, from whose face the earth and the heaven fled away; and there was found no place for them.*
[12] *And I saw the dead, small and great, stand before God; and **the books were opened**: and **another book was opened, which is the book of life**: and **the dead were judged out of those things which were written in the books, according to their works***

[13] *And the sea gave up the dead which were in it; and death and hell delivered up the dead which were in them: and they were judged every man according to their works.*
[14] *And death and hell were cast into the lake of fire.* ***This is the second death.***
[15] *And whosoever was not found written in the **book of life** was cast into the lake of fire.* Revelation 20: 11-15

Revelation 20: 11-15 is an amazing statement of what will come to pass as the 1000-year Millennial Kingdom comes to a close. The *Great White Throne Judgment* is the last judgment of man which will take place before eternity begins. A myth needs to be destroyed concerns those who will be judged. All prophecy teachers identify the Great White Throne Judgment as a judgment of unbelievers. These are unbelievers from all age's past, including the Millennial Kingdom. However, there are others. The Great White Throne Judgment will involve three main classes of people: (1) Unbelievers from all age's past, from Adam and Eve to the end of the Millennial Kingdom (2) non-believers that are either alive (Revelation 20: 7-9) or have died during the 1000-year Millennial Kingdom … II Corinthians 5:10, Revelation 20: 1-13 and (3) All true believers that are either alive or have died during the Millennial Kingdom.

There are several *books* which will be opened at this judgment (Revelation 20:12). One is called the *Book of Life*. It appears that a book has been kept by God throughout all 7 dispensations of time which is called the Book of Life. It is *conjectured* that before the world was created God possessed a Book that contained all of the names of every person who would ever be born (Revelation 3:5, Philippians 4:3, Revelation 21:27). When a person dies *without* ever believing that God would send a redeemer to forgive all sins (Old Testament) or accepting Jesus Christ as their Lord and Savior and the Son of God (New Covenant); their name is erased from the Book of Life. This is final and irreversible. Those whose names are found in the Book of Life will enter into the eternal Kingdom of God, and those whose name is not found in the Book of Life will be cast into the Lake of Burning Fire. A question often asked is: *How are little children saved before the age of reason?* If a baby or a child dies *before* the age of reason, their name is not erased from the Book of Life and there will be a special place for them in heaven. Those whose names are not found in the Book of Life are cast into the Lake of Burning Fire and experience eternal separation from God the Father and God the Son. This is called the *second death* (Revelation 20:14). What is contained in the *other books* (Revelation 20:12) is pure speculation, but it is *proposed* that all unbelievers will be held accountable for all sins that they have committed in the flesh as unbelievers. These sins were forgiven by the blood of Jesus on the Cross of calvary, but all unbelievers have died in unbelief and refused the Grace of God will be asked why they did those things. Note carefully that since calvary, sins committed in the flesh will not condemn unbelievers. However, at the final judgment of unbelievers, their individual choice of belief or unbelief will be reflected in their deeds… Rewards for believers and punishment for unbelievers.

[3] *… thinkest thou this, O man, that judges them which do such things, and doest do the same, that thou shalt escape the judgment of God?*
[4] *Or despise the riches of his goodness and forbearance and longsuffering; not knowing* that *the goodness of God leads to repentance?*
[5] *But after thy hardness and impenitent heart treasures up unto thyself wrath against the day of wrath and revelation of the righteous judgment of God;*
[6] **Who will render to every man according to his deeds**   Romans 2: 3-6

If this is to be literally interpreted, it raises an interesting possibility. There *may* be degrees of torment for those who have been cast into the Lake of Burning Fire. This is pure speculation based upon Revelation 20:12.

There is only one way that all sinful men and women from all 7 dispensations can be saved and awarded eternal life… That is by the sacrificial death of Jesus Christ. When Christ died on the Cross of Calvary, He died for the sins of every human who would ever live…. Past, present and future. As part of the eternal Godhead, Jesus Christ existed before the world was formed. He was present throughout the 1st five dispensations with God the Father and in the 6th dispensation he became the Son of Man when he came to redeem sin and offer eternal life to all who would believe that He was the son of God. He made a *public spectacle* of Satan (Colossians 2:15), defeated death by his resurrection from the grave and now sits upon the right hand of God the Father awaiting His second advent. Adam and Eve knew that He would come to redeem them from sin; Noah and his family knew that he would come to redeem them from sin; Abraham, Joseph and all of the patriarchs knew that He would come to redeem them from sin; and those Jews who lived under the law and died in the faith of Abraham knew that God would send a prophesied redeemer to save them from their sins. Jesus Christ was that promised Messiah who never sinned, completely fulfilled every jot and tittle of the law (Matthew 5:18) and died for the sins of man. He who knew no sin took the sins of the entire world upon himself. He offered Himself as the perfect, sacrificial Lamb of God. The law was finished… salvation by works was finished… and the issue of sin as a barrier to salvation and eternal life was settled. Every man or woman who would ever walk upon this earth would not only carry into this life the original sin of Adam, but all would sin in this life. A sinless life was impossible both before the law, under the law and after the law. Sin had to be completely removed as a barrier to eternal life. That is why Christ offered Himself as the final, complete and perfect sacrifice under the law. From Adam and Eve to the end of the Millennial kingdom, sin is no longer a barrier to eternal life and salvation.

Under the law, there were only two classes of people: Jews and Gentiles. The Jews were selected by God to be his chosen people, and they were given a set of written laws by which to live. *What about the Gentiles?*

The gentiles were viewed by the Jews as evil… idolators… and heathen. Many teach that the Gentiles could not be saved under the law, but this appears to be a false assumption. The law was given to Israel to follow so that they would be set them apart as a peculiar people who would glorify God. They were to be circumcised to identify them as people chosen by God. But this did not mean that the Gentiles (all other people) could not be saved. God told the Jews:

when a stranger (Gentile) *shall sojourn with thee, and will keep the Passover to the LORD, let all his males be circumcised, and then let him come near and keep it; and he shall be as one that is born in the land*   Genesis 12:48

In Luke 7:1-9 Jesus heals a Gentile friend of a centurion because of his many blessings he bestowed upon the nation of Israel, including building a Jewish synagogue. After this event Jesus replied regarding this Gentile:

…I say unto you, I have not found so great faith, no, not in Israel   Luke 7:9

God's Word says that: *For by grace are ye saved through faith; and that not of yourselves: it is the gift of God* (Ephesians 2:8). Grace means that God loves, forgives, and saves us not because of who we are or what we do but because of the work of Jesus Christ. Faith is knowing that God is true to His word, and that He cannot lie. *Faith is being sure of what we hope for and certain of what we do not see* (Hebrews 11:1). Before the law, after the law was given and after the work of Christ on the Cross of calvary there was only one way…*by faith*. Faith that Christ had died for the forgiveness of sin. Remember that Christ was born under the law, lived under the law and died under the law. Before

Calvary, there were only Jews and Gentiles. After calvary there are only believers and nonbelievers.

The Righteousness of God

The average Christian today is familiar with the word *righteous* and the term *righteousness of God*; but how can this foundational attribute of God be clearly explained? Websters Dictionary defines righteous as being *morally right and justified*. However, when one speaks of the righteousness of God this simple definition is totally inadequate. The righteousness of God is more than being morally correct, it is who and what He is. the divine attribute that describes God as acting always in a way that is consistent with his own character. God is pure and inherently righteous. Not only does it define his own actions and laws for mankind, he demands righteousness in those he calls his sons and daughters, he provides righteousness in abundance, and he rewards those who seek to follow after Him as a righteous and faithful servant. God's holy word consistently reflects the righteousness of God, and declares that *righteousness and justice* are the foundation of God's throne (Psalms 89:14). What is the purpose of a foundation? Any home builder will tell you that without a firm foundation, no house or building can survive for long. Luke said that anyone who would come to him and seek wisdom, understanding and righteousness would be like a house built upon a firm foundation.

[48] *He is like a man which built a house, and dug deep, and laid the* ***foundation*** *on a rock: and when the flood arose, the stream beat vehemently upon that house, and could not shake it: for it was founded upon a rock.*
[49] *But he that heareth, and doeth not, is like a man that without a* ***foundation*** *built an house upon the earth; against which the stream did beat vehemently, and immediately it fell; and the ruin of that house was great*   Luke 11: 48-49

Righteousness is essential to his very being and characterizes all that he does: God *is* morally and ethically *right*, and he *acts* only in keeping with what is right and just. That is, he is right, just, and true. Paradoxically, there is no Christian who is totally righteous in God's sight. Paul said it this way: *As it is written, there is none righteous, no, not one* (Romans 3:10). All righteousness in man comes from God. Whatever righteousness is found in anyone comes from God. Righteousness cannot be earned... it is imputed to us by grace through faith. Abraham was justified before God because: *Abraham believed God, and it was counted unto him for righteousness* (Romans 4:3). Access to God's righteousness is attained by believing upon His Son.

That as sin hath reigned unto death, even so might grace reign through righteousness unto eternal life by Jesus Christ our Lord   Romans 5:21

[20] *Now then we are ambassadors for Christ, as though God did beseech you by us: we pray you in Christ's stead, be ye reconciled to God.*
[21] **For he hath made him to be sin for us, who knew no sin; that we might be made the righteousness of God in him**   II Corinthians 5: 20-21

If righteousness defines the nature and character of God, how can God be a God of Wrath? Paul addressed this question in his letter to the Romans.

[16] *For I am not ashamed of the gospel of Christ: for it is the power of God unto salvation to everyone that believes; to the Jew first, and also to the Greek.*
[17] *For therein is the righteousness of God revealed from faith to faith: as it is written: The just shall live by faith.*
[18] *For the wrath of God is revealed from heaven against all ungodliness and unrighteousness of men, who hold the truth in unrighteousness*
Romans 1: 16-18

Paul clearly explains that all righteousness comes to man from God, and is accessed through faith in Jesus Christ. Righteous is imputed to every Christian, and cannot be obtained by reading the scriptures, doing good deeds or preaching the everlasting gospel. It is a gift from God. if righteousness is the essence and character of God, then unrighteousness is an attribute of all unbelievers. For those who deny His son Jesus Christ, God is justified in executing His Wrath (Romans 1:18). If man chooses to follow Satan and sin, God will respond in His wrath.

> unrighteousness anywhere is a threat to righteousness everywhere. The minute we begin condoning evil, justifying our selfishness, and excusing our pet sins, instead of repenting of them, we are asking for judgment: for blindness, darkness, waywardness, folly, debased minds, and perverse passions.   Martin Luther King

[8] *Now as Jannes and Jambres withstood Moses, so do these also resist the truth: men of corrupt minds, reprobate concerning the faith.*
[9] *But they shall proceed no further: for their folly shall be manifest unto all men, as theirs also was*   II Timothy 3:9

Because God is both good and just, he will punish sin. The worst kind of judgment he can give is to give us up to whatever our sinful passions desire. The Lord and His Son Jesus Christ both understand how man is inherently prone to sin.it is only through his Grace and love and through the Holy Spirit that dwells within us can each of us expect to avoid the Wrath of God.

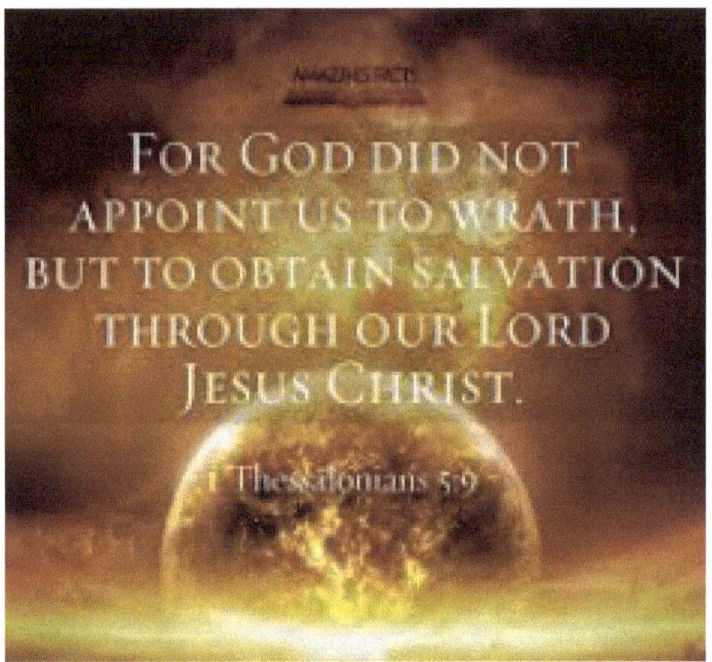

Chapter 3
Judgments and Wrath of God in the Old Testament

In Chapter 1 seven dispensations of time were introduced. The first 4 dispensations of time covered the time span of the Old Testament between when Adam and Eve were placed into the Garden of Eden (Dispensation of Innocence) and the nation of Israel was liberated by God after 215 years of slavery in Egypt (Disposition of New Beginnings). During this period of time God ruled over man in a theocracy. There was no written law, but man inherently knew right from wrong and it is clear that God had personally told man what He demanded if they were to avoid His wrath (Cain and Abel, Nimrod and the Tower of Babel).

Throughout the Scriptures, God's Wrath is poured out upon those who are in rebellion against him. The rebellion against God by man as found in scriptures is much more serious than rebellion of man against man. Rebellion against God always involves sinful acts against a sinless God. God is holy and cannot tolerate sin in any form. His anger against man who ignore his laws, statutes and commands is more that righteous indignation and punitive response. He is morally, religiously and righteously a pure and sinless God.

This leads to a dilemma which has disturbed and confounded Christians since time began. There are degrees of righteous indignation and God' Wrath which cannot be explained. God struck down and consumed Nadab and Abihu with fire for simply offering unauthorized incense in the Holy Place, but He only banned Cain to a life by himself in the wilderness for murdering his brother and then trying to lie his way out of it. The first recorded instance of God's wrath against sin was before Adam and Eve were created.

The Dateless Past: The Fallen Angels
When Adam and Eve were cast out of the Garden of Eden, they began to populate the earth. Men and women were not created by a great cosmic explosion or random act of nature, but they were made by God and all men and women came from the seed of Adam. Man with a soul did not evolve from apes, but were created in the image of God as complete humans. This does not deny that when God scattered man across this earth as a result of Nimrod wanting to be like God and build a towering ziggurat which reached skyward, people were scattered across the earth by God and spoke different languages. This does not negate, dilute or deny evolution as different tribes evolved separately and adopted to their new environment.

Before God created Adam and Eve, the *Archangel Satan* ruled over all of the angels that God had created. He was the *anointed cherub* who was also known as *Lucifer*. The only time that Lucifer appears in the King James English bible is in Isaiah 14:12. When the original Hebrew text was translated into Latin, the word *Lucifero* was used. When the King James English version of the Latin text emerged in 1611, *Lucifero* was translated as *Lucifer*. Lucifer became so impressed with his own beauty, intelligence, power, and position that he began to desire for himself the honor and glory that belonged to God alone. This rebellion against God resulted in Lucifer being cast out of Heaven (Isaiah 14:12) and he was not alone… 1/3 of all the angels that God had created were cast out with him (Revelation 12: 3-4). As a result of his rebellion against God, Lucifer was banished from living in heaven (Isaiah 14:12). He became corrupt, and his name was changed from Lucifer… which means *morning star*… to Satan… which means *adversary*. Lucifer was responsible for the beginning of sin in the universe when he became jealous of God and wanted to be worshipped as God. Strangely enough, when Lucifer was banished from heaven, 1/3 of all the Holy Angels that God had created went with him (Revelation 12). These fallen angels became what we now call *demons*. Demons are fallen angels and spirit beings who seek to find a body that they can live in and control.

Regardless of the reason for retribution and severity which God takes against sin and disobedience, God's anger and punitive action towards sin is real and often deadly. Noah's Flood (Genesis 6–9), the destruction of Sodom and Gomorrah (Genesis 19), the defeat of Pharaoh and his army in the Red Sea (Exodus 14–15), and the death of 3000 Israelites at Mt. Sinai (Exodus 34:2) are all examples of God destroying sinful men. God cannot forgive sin, and while he may delay justice he cannot compromise or deny his holiness. This is the theological basis of the sacrificial death of Jesus Christ His Son upon the Cross of Calvary. God cannot forgive or tolerate sin, so in His divine wisdom he sent Jesus Christ to die for the sins of the entire world. Without that plan for the forgiveness of sins, no one could ever attain eternal life in God's Kingdom. We will discuss this further in Chapter 4 when God's judgment and wrath in the New Testament is discussed.

After the Cross, salvation and eternal life in God's Kingdom is given by *Grace* and *Faith*. A major part of salvation by faith is the impact of sin on man after the Cross of Calvary. What exactly did it mean that Christ paid the price, and sacrificed His own sinless life for those who could not save themselves? When Christ died and became the perfect, sinless sacrifice for all sin…...past, present and future, his blood was the supreme and final offering that satisfied God's holy wrath against sin, so that those who put their trust in Christ could have forgiveness of sins. God did not compromise His holiness when the sin issue was settled by Christ, but He can righteously forgive those who recognize their sin and come to Him for mercy. This does not mean that man will not be required to answer for acts of sin and disobedience; it simply means that those acts will result in a loss of rewards and authority in the eternal Kingdom of God. It also means that Believers may, and do, experience discipline from the hand of God… and even tribulation and persecution in this life. But tribulation is intended to help us to grow and mature in faith, and teaches us that sinful acts will not be ignored. Every person will be held accountable for what they say and do when they stand before the Judgment Seat of God. Under the New Covenant, no man will be condemned to eternal separation from God based upon sinful acts or behavior. Only one question will be asked: *What did you do with my Son? Did you believe that He died for your sins and did you accept Him as your Lord and Savior?*

Throughout the Scriptures, you find a division between God's wrath directed towards sinners and His love toward all mankind…...saints and sinners alike. His wrath was poured out on the people of Noah's time by the waters of a great flood, but righteous Noah and his family were all spared. Judgment was levied against Sodom and Gomorrah, but Lot and his family was spared. Egypt was beset by 10 plagues, but the descendants of Abraham were not harmed. Over and over again we see this repeated in the Old Testament. When God sent His only Son as the final and perfect sacrifice for all sins, those who come to the Father by love and grace will not necessarily become exempt from tribulation in this life, but they will escape the Wrath of God.

One of the things that was discovered as this book was being written is how the Wrath of God in the Old Testament was in stark contrast to how the Wrath of God was manifested in the New Testament. If one carefully studies the Old Testament, it will become obvious that it was not rare to read how God poured out His Wrath upon Jews and Gentiles alike in righteous indignation. This was true in all five dispensations which preceded the current Dispensation of Grace. However, you will search the scriptures in vain to find God descending to this earth and releasing His wrath upon anyone for sinful acts under the New Covenant. The lone exceptions to this rule are the three judgments at which all men and women must appear at the end of this Dispensation of Grace (*Bema Seat Judgment*, *Judgment of the Nations* and the *Great White Throne Judgment*). We will discuss these in Chapter 4. Finally, note that it is not in the eternal plan of God to judge man as He did in the Old Testament as He now does under the New Covenant. God has honored His Son by placing Him in charge of all judgment, since it was by His sacrificial death on the Cross of Calvary that the sins of all true believers can be forgiven.

[31] *Behold, the days come, saith the LORD, that I will make a new covenant with the house of Israel, and with the house of Judah:*
[32] *Not according to the covenant that I made with their fathers in the day that I took them by the hand to bring them out of the land of Egypt; which my covenant they brake, although I was an husband unto them, saith the LORD*
Jeremiah 31: 31-34

For the Father judges no man, but hath committed all judgment unto the Son
John 5:22

We will have more to say about this later.

This has only been a brief discussion of how the judgment and Wrath of God is consistent and justified by the holiness of God. Books have been written on this topic, and it is not the intention of this book to fully explore this important topic. Several examples of how the judgment and Wrath of God was manifested in the Old Testament will now be presented. Chapter 5 will be directed to the Wrath of God under the New Covenant

The Dispensation of Innocence

The *Dispensation of Innocence* was the period of time during which Adam and Eve lived in the Garden of Eden. Initially, there was no knowledge of sin. God had given them instructions on what to eat and what to do, but the only thing He commanded them *not* to do was to never eat of the fruit of the tree of the knowledge of good and evil. This command from God was serious, and He declared that the penalty of violating His law was death. When Adam and Eve both sinned, they were expunged from the Garden of Eden and they began to die (Genesis 2:17). This was the first time that God pronounced judgment upon man. He cast them out of the Garden and declared that Eve and all women to follow her would experience pain and suffering in childberth. Because Adam had failed God by not protecting Eve against Satan, God cursed the ground and brought forth thistles and thorns. Adam and His progeny would no longer be sustained by fruit whch grew abundantly in the Garden of Eden, but Man would now have to grow his own food, till and work the ground, and labor in the field by the sweat of his brow (Genesis 3: 17-20). This judgment and punishment of Adam and Eve was not called the Wrath of God, but it certainly was. It is interesting and disasterous that all of the things that resulted from their acts of sin were not just pronounced upon Adam and eve, but they were propogated upon every man and woman who would be born from the seed of Adam. From that point on, *all* men and women were doomed to physical death because of the sin of one man… Adam. God is so opposed to all sin and the sin nature that He could not forgive and forget that Adam and Eve had chosen sin over holiness…Satan over God. They had chosen their own personal will and desires over the soverignty of God. *The wages of sin is death* (Romans 6:23). All men from that point in time forward would pay for the sin of one man.

However, in the eternal plan of God He had a plan to redeem mankind and forgive their sins. This is the great work of Jesus Christ on the Cross of Calvary. He willingly shed His precious blood for the sins of all mankind from Adam to the Final Judgment. Jesus Christ was the perfect and pure Lamb of God that was Crucified and ascended to heaven, being accepted as the perfect, eternal sacrifice for sin on the Feast of Firstfruits after spending 3 nights and 3 days in the grave.

For he (God the father) *hath made him* (Jesus Christ the Son) *to be sin for us, who knew no sin; that we might be made the righteousness of God in him*
II Corinthians 5:21

For he hath made him to be sin for us, who knew no sin; that we might be made the righteousness of God in him   Colossians 1: 19-21

The Nephilim

In some strange and unbelievable way, there was another rebellion in heaven which must have taken place between the *Dispensation of Innocence* and the *Dispensation of Conscience*. According to the apostle Matthew: *At the resurrection people will neither marry nor be given in marriage; they will be like the angels in heaven* (Matthew 22:30). As the earth began to be populated, the female offspring of Adam and Eve were beautiful to behold and a group of angels in heaven noticed their beauty.

[1] *And it came to pass, when men began to multiply on the face of the earth, and daughters were born unto them,*
[2] *That the **sons of God** saw the daughters of men that they were fair; and they took them wives of all which they chose*   Genesis 6: 1-2

Who were theses *sons of God*? Ancient Jewish Rabbis wrote that these were angels who descended upon the earth and had sexual relations with women. The offspring of these incestuous relationships were further identified as a race of giants called *Nephilim*. Nephilim was an ancient Hebrew word for *giants*… it does not occur in the bible. This conjecture is supported by a mysterious record in the Book of Jude.

[6] *And the angels which kept not their first estate, but left their own habitation, he hath reserved in everlasting chains under darkness unto the judgment of the great day.*
[7] *Even as Sodom and Gomorrah, and the cities about them in like manner, giving themselves over to fornication, and going after **strange flesh**, are set forth for an example, **suffering the vengeance of eternal fire***   Jude 1: 6-7

These offspring of angels and women were mentioned again when the spies which were sent by Moses returned from their exploratory mission of the land of Canaan. They reported that: *the people who dwell in the land are strong; the cities are fortified and very large; moreover, we saw the descendants of Anak there*

(Numbers 13:28). The Anakin were described as a race of giants (Genesis 6: 1-4) who *descended from Anak* according to the Old Testament (Jude 1: 6-7). They were said to have lived in the southern part of the land of Canaan, near Hebron (Genesis. 23:2; Joshua 15:13). According to extra-biblical sources these were the race of giants which the spies saw in the land of Canaan. The size of these giants can only be conjectured, but it is recorded that Goliath, a warrior from the Philistine camp, stood about 9 feet 9 inches tall and wore a coat of armor weighing some 125 pounds. Og, who was king of Bashan, slept on an iron bed 14 feet long and 6 feet wide. A warrior named Benaiah who fought with King David defeated a large Egyptian soldier in battle who was about 7' 6" tall (I Chronicles 11:23).

There were obviously giants in the Land of Canaan after the flood, but were the giants that were seen by the spies sent by Moses the descendants of fallen angels? It is the opinion of this author that they were. Whatever men were called *giants* in the Land of Canaan also lived before the flood, and they were all drowned in that great deluge. So how did these giants still exist in the land of Canaan? It is possible that their supernatural genes survived the flood through Noah and one or more of his three sons. If so, they might have eventually caused a race of giants to emerge. However, there is no definitive biblical record to support this conclusion. We only know that there were giants in the land of Canaan hundreds of years after the flood. We best not declare biblical proof without solid evidence. We do know, however, that regardless of what the physical offspring of these angels might have looked like, God was not pleased with the angels who rebelled against Him because of lust and immoral behavior. They were incarcerated in a special dungeon which is contained in the depths of the earth called *Tartarus* (2 Peter 2:4, Jude 1:6) which is said to be a place of total darkness.

And the angels which kept not their first estate, but left their own habitation, he hath reserved in everlasting chains under darkness unto the judgment of the great day. Jude 6

[4] *For if God spared not the angels that sinned, but cast them down to* **hell** (Tartarus), *and delivered them into chains of darkness, to be reserved unto judgment* II Peter 2: 4

God was so full of Wrath that He cast all of the fallen angels who produced earthly offspring into a subterranean dungeon called *Tartarus* (mistranslated as *hell* in II Peter 2:4) where they await final judgment. These angelic beings will be judged for their sinful behavior… perhaps by the saints (I Corinthians 6:3), but the fate of 1/3 of the heavenly host which were defeated along with Satan at the Battle of Armageddon is not revealed in the Holy Scriptures. It is *conjectured* and proposed that all of these fallen angels will be judged together, and the only time that this can occur is at the Great White Throne Judgment which will follow the 1000- year Millennial Kingdom.

The Dispensation of Conscience

The Dispensation of Conscience started when Adam and Eve were cast out of the Garden of Eden, and it ended when God destroyed all mankind except for Noah and his family with a great flood. It is called the *Dispensation of Conscince* because there was no written law. However, just because there was no written law does not mean that man could not discerne the difference between good or evil. Athough not generally recognized, before Adam and Eve sinned there was no knowledge of good or evil…..only good. God Himself called all that He had made in Genesis 1 and Genesis 2, *good*. It was not until both ate of the forbidden fruit that man was cursed by self judgment and guilt when sinful acts were committed. Each individual… Christian or unbeliever… Jew or Gentile… is born with a knowledge of what is good or evil. Since God punished man for sinful deeds, He must have told them what was sinful to Him and what was not. The most important change which took place is that Adam and his progeny knew the difference between good and evil, and every person who followed Adam and Eve were born into this world with a body and mind that is already prone to acts of sin. It is important to understand that after the *fall* of Adam and Eve, God communicated with man and told them what was sinful in His eyes and how to avoid being overcome by Satan. A classic example is the story of Cain and Abel. Cain killed his brother out of jealously when God preferred Abel's gift to the Lord over his own. When Cain killed his brother Abel, He lied to God and tried to create excuses for what he had done. The sinful act of Cain was just the beginning. Cain *had* to know the difference between good and evil acts when He killed his brother and lied about it. Some men were drawn to evil and sin just as they are today because they love creation more than the creator, and as their number grew all the world became more and more rebellious and sinful until God had enough.

[5] And GOD saw that the wickedness of man was great in the earth, and that every imagination of the thoughts of his heart was only evil continually.
[6] And it repented the LORD that he had made man on the earth, and it grieved him at his heart.
[7] And the LORD said, I will destroy man whom I have created from the face of the earth; both man, and beast, and the creeping thing, and the fowls of the air; for it repenteth me that I have made them.
[8] But Noah found grace in the eyes of the LORD.   Genesis 6: 5-8

But Noah found grace….

The following pages will introduce and discuss several biblical accounts of God's judgment and wrath during the Dispensation of Conscience. As we examine and discuss scriptural accounts, keep in mind that there was no written law and God was the sole ruler over the people in a theocracy.

In the New Testament, Paul revealed the following truth.

[12] Wherefore, as by one man sin entered into the world, and death by sin: So, death passed upon all men, for all have sinned:
[13] (For until the law sin was in the world: but sin is not imputed when there is no law.
[14] Nevertheless death reigned from Adam to Moses, even over them that had not sinned after the similitude of Adam's transgression, who is the figure of him that was to come   Romans 5: 12-14

Romans 5:13 has been an object of confusion and investigation ever since Paul wrote it. In Romans Chapters 1-5 Paul addresses the subject of sin and the effects of sin from Adam to the current Age of Grace. Paul compared salvation under the law (of Moses) to salvation by faith and grace by which all men (Jews and gentiles) are now justified by the blood of Jesus Christ. This contrast comes to a head in Romans 5. In Romans 5: 1-11 a brilliant summary is given concerning how Jesus Christ has rescued us from death and sin. In Romans 5:9:

Much more then, being now justified by his blood, we shall be saved from wrath through him   Romans 5:9

In Romans 5, Paul shifts His message of love and grace to both Jews and Gentiles by addressing time past (the first 5 dispensations) and how sin and death ruled over unrighteous men. First, he observes that the original sin of Adam brought death. From the moment that Adam and Eve sinned, they began to die. This was *physical* death which would not be experienced by Adam and Eve as long as they ate fruit from the Tree of Life (Genesis 2:9). There was also no *spiritual death* until Adam and Eve sinned. They walked and talked with God and in the cool of the evening until God banned Him from his physical presence.

[12] *Wherefore, as by one man sin entered into the world, and death by sin; and so death passed upon all men, for that all have sinned*   Romans 5:12

The wages of sin bring death. When Adam sinned, all men were doomed to a physical death, and all men died in unforgiven sin until Jesus Christ defeated both sin and death on the Cross of Calvary. Paul is not addressing physical death in Romans 5:12 but spiritual death. That death is called the 2nd death in Revelation 20: 13-14, and it cannot be overcome by righteousness and righteous living; This is because we are all born in sin by the fall of Adam (Romans 5:12). Only the blood of Christ can save us from spiritual death. Paul continues….

[13] *(For until the law sin was in the world: but sin is not imputed when there is no law.*
[14] *Nevertheless death reigned from Adam to Moses, even over them that had not sinned after the similitude of Adam's transgression, who is the figure of him that was to come*   Romans 5: 13-14

This is one of the most difficult passages in the New Testament. Adam committed the original sin by ignoring the command (law) of God. This was confirmed by Paul in Romans 5:14. But, then in Romans 5: 13 he clearly wrote that sin is not imputed when there is no law. Most biblical scholars relate this to the written law of Moses, but this is obviously not true. There was sin in the world both before and after Adam and Eve sinned, so there obviously was law, and it must have been spoken to man by God. This is confirmed in Romans 5:14a: *Nevertheless, death reigned from Adam to Moses.* Paul continues to say that *death reigned* even though the sin of man was not the same as Adams sin. Clearly, there were unwritten Laws of God that had been broken.

Paul clearly said that even though the sons of Adam did not sin just as Adam did, they were still going to die a physical death as a result of Adam's single transgression. So up until the giving of the Law to Moses: *Was Adam was only the man who had sinned*? The answer is clearly...No... and yet death reigned over all men because death passed from Adam to all his progeny. It is evident that sin was in the world even though the written law had not yet been given by God. Physical death came upon many not due to natural causes but as a penalty for sin (Sodom and Gomorrah). Hence, sin *must* have been known to man even if there was no written law.

For as many as have sinned without law shall also perish without law: and as many as have sinned in the law shall be judged by the law   Romans 2:12

This is proof that there was sin in the world before written laws, and that it is possible to perish without written laws. Paul confirmed that this was the case between Adam and Mt. Sinai.

[14] *For when the Gentiles, which have not the law, do by nature the things contained in the law, these, having not the law, are a law unto themselves:*
[15] *Which shew the work of the law written in their hearts, their conscience also bearing witness, and their thoughts the mean while accusing or else excusing one another;)*   Romans 2:14-15

Those who sinned against God before the Law of Moses did not violate any written law because there was none. They either went against their conscience or against God's spoken laws (Romans 1: 18-32). Even though the flesh is dominated by the sin nature inherited from Adam, man inherently knows right from wrong. They sinned in the same way that Adam did by breaking a stated law of God. This is evident by recall of what Adam and Eve did after they had sinned. They hid from the Lord and Adam made weak excuses... They both knew that they had sinned. Romans 5:13 *does not* mean that people did not sin. They did. But they did not break any written law, for it had not yet been given.

The law in Romans 5:14 was not the Law of Moses which was given to the Nation of Israel by God at Mt. Sinai. The Greek word for imputed is *ellogeo*. It is a legal term which means to *assign to an account*. Paul is stating that where there is no law, a man or woman cannot be charged with a transgression of law. From Adam to Moses there was no *written* law; no 10 commandments in writing which could be transgressed; and no acts of sin could be charged to an account which did not exist. The paradox is that this chapter will describe several incidents in which God brought death upon those who ignored his holy commands. There were transgressions against God, and there was sin, and there was death. Since God executed righteous judgment and wrath upon those who transgressed against his holy commands, there must have been laws which were disobeyed by man. *Does the holy Bible support this conjecture?*

The answer to this question relates to God's nature, His revelation and our response. Biblically speaking, God is holy, just, unchanging and all-loving. It is obvious that He is also a God of Judgment and Wrath when His commands are violated. This means that God will always do what is just and right. When it comes to God's revelation, we can divide these into three categories: (1) *special* (2) *general* and (3) *natural* revelations. His *special revelation* includes the Bible and his commandments which are personally given. These are both a direct and special means of God revealing Himself to individuals. *General revelation*, is revelation of who God is and is not as revealed in the Holy Scriptures. *Natural revelation*, consists of what God has revealed of Himself via the natural world and moral conscience. Even pagan societies believe in some sort of God(s) which can be benevolent or punitive. Two passages in Romans further explain this general revelation:

*For since the creation of the world God's invisible qualities – his eternal power and divine nature – have been clearly seen, being understood from what has been made, so that **men are without excuse*** Romans 1:20

[14] *For when the Gentiles, which have not the law, do by nature the things contained in the law, these, **having not the law, are a law unto themselves**:*
[15] *Which shew the work of the law **written in their hearts**, their conscience also bearing witness, and **their thoughts** the mean while accusing or else excusing one another* Romans 2: 14-15

> The requirements of the law are *written on their hearts*. Romans 2:15 reveals that everyone has an inherent knowledge of God, that this
> was *clearly* known from creation (Romans 1:20), and that *everyone* also has a God-given moral compass.   Robert Valarde

Abraham obeyed my voice, and kept my charge, my commandments, my statutes, and my laws   Genesis 26:5

Genesis 26:5 was written thousands of years before God gave His written laws to Moses and the Nation of Israel.

The concept of God as a *God of Wrath* is not readily accepted by many Christians. How can a God who is the embodiment of love also rule and reign as a God of Wrath? Man should never question and can rarely understand the ways of God because man cannot fully relate to His holiness, love and mercy. But we can understand that even though God is longsuffering and desires that no one should perish, His Judgment and Wrath are justified and a part of His holiness.

Adam and Eve

Almost every Christian and many non-Christians can recite the story of Adam and Eve. However, when Adam and Eve were expelled from the Garden of Eden that was only part of the Wrath of God. When both were driven from the garden, God declared more of His wrath against all involved.

(1) Both Adam and Eve were told before they both sinned that in the day that the fruit was eaten, *they would surely die*. Obviously, they did not die on that faithful day. The correct interpretation is that they would forfeit their immortality in the Garden and would begin to die on that day. Adam lived 930 years, and w4e are not told the age of Eve when she died but she had a child at age 130.

(2) Eve was the 1st to be tempted and sin, and she did not escape God's wrath. God told Eve that she (and every woman) would increase her sorrow (pain) in childbirth.

(3) Evidently, Adam and Eve lived in the Garden as co-equals. God told Eve that from the point she left the garden Adam would *rule over thee* (Genesis 3:16).

Adam also felt the Wrath of God. God told Adam:

(1) Adam had all the food (fruit) that he could eat in the Garden, but from the point he was forced to leave God cursed the ground and told Adam that he would have to *till* (Plant) *the soil*, and by extension harvest whatever was planted and pick whatever was to be eaten.

(2) The earth would need to be cultivated and prepared for planting because it would be full of thistles and thorns.

(3) Bread could be eaten, but it would not be easy to create (Genesis 3:19).

The snake which was inhabited by Satan did not escape the Wrath of God.

(1) Evidently the serpent which tempted Eve was beautiful in appearance and Eve had no fear of that reptile. It is obvious that a snake of almost any kind is not admired and is feared today.

(2) The serpent which *beguiled* Eve in the garden was cursed above all other beasts of the earth (Genesis 3:14) and all cattle. It must have stood upright as it tempted Eve, because: *Upon thy belly shalt thou go, and dust shalt thou eat all the days of thy life:*

Even though God poured His wrath out upon Adam and Eve, Grace did still abound. God made them both *coats of skins, and clothed them* (Genesis 3:21).

After Adam and Eve were driven from the Garden of Eden they began to procreate and repopulate the world as God had commanded them. The earth began to be filled with the sons and daughters of Adam, and they migrated to many different lands. The following observations concerning how mankind grew and prospered are gratefully taken from the works of Robert Gibbs.

> There are not a lot of details about Adam and Eve after they were expelled from the Garden of Eden, but we can glean some things from the scriptures which tell us about what they experienced in their lifetimes.
>
> Adam and Eve lived a hard life outside the Garden of Eden. Jehovah had cursed the ground because of their rebellion against him, and thorns and thistles choked their gardens and fields. With sweat and hard work, they toiled to eke out a living from the soil. They knew they were reaping the consequences of their decision to disobey God and forfeit their personal friendship with their generous Creator.
>
> They had forfeited their intimate relationship with God, and without the fruit of the Tree of Life, they started to die…. gradually growing older and losing their perfect health. All of their children were born after God put them out of the garden. Their children inherited

imperfection and sinful tendencies from the seed of Adam, and they too would gradually grow old and die.

Adam and Eve had many sons and daughters. God had told Eve: *In pain you will give birth to children*, but despite her pain, what a delight it must have been when Eve gave birth to their first-born son, Cain and again with the birth of a second son, Abel. Little did they know the wrenching heartache which would come.

Imagine the devastating pain they must have experienced when their first-born son brutally murdered his younger brother. After Cain killed his brother God banished him sending him far away from the rest of his family. In time Cain somehow married, and his wife had children. As people multiplied the selfish, evil nature of Cain brought increased violence and sin. One of Cain's descendants boasted with pride of being even more violent and vengeful than Cain!

In the third generation, a new evil arose. No doubt with Satan's influence, people began calling on the name of Jehovah, not as act of pure worship, but evidently using God's sacred name in a blasphemous, disrespectful way in the corrupt form of a new religion (Genesis 4:8, 23-26).

Adam lived for 930 years, and when he was 622 years old Enoch was born. The world was becoming more and more morally and spiritually corrupt, and violence was everywhere. Enoch was a God-fearing man, and he prophesied that God would destroy all sinful and ungodly men.

The Bible does not tell us how long Eve lived, but she likely lived the kind of long life which Adam lived. In their lifetimes they witness the selfish, corrupt, violent world to which they had given birth.

As Adam and Eve grew old and approach death, they realized what a monstrous lie with which Satan had tempted Eve: *you certainly will not die* if you eat this fruit, asserting that God had lied to them about the consequence of disobedience. Satan also implied that they would be *better* and as smart as God by refusing to obey the only command which He had given them. They saw with their own eyes what a lie that had been as well.

Mankind was not better off; life was hard and unforgiving outside the beautiful, bountiful, garden home they had lost, and they watched as the world descended deeper and deeper into godlessness and violence.

Just three generations after Adam's death the Bible says: *And GOD saw that the wickedness of man was great in the earth, and that every imagination of the thoughts of his heart was only evil continually* (Genesis 6:5). So, God told Noah: *behold, I, even I, do bring a flood of waters upon the earth, to destroy all flesh, wherein is the breath of life, from under heaven; and everything that is in the earth shall die* (Genesis 6:17). Only three generations after Adam's death things had become so bad that God was moved to destroyed that wicked violent generation and give mankind a new start with the sons of Noah.

Robert Gibbs: A student of theology and a Retired Christian minister

Cain and Abel

Adam and Eve had been expunged from the Garden of Eden for disobeying God and committing the first sin. God was no longer walking and talking with Adam and Eve because sin had destroyed their relationship to one another. Adam and Eve began to populate the world and it appears from the Holy records that Cain was the first man to have born into a sin-corrupted world. Shortly after Cain was born, Eve had a 2nd son who she named Abel (Genesis 4: 1-2). As the two boys grew to maturity, Cain became a farmer who tilled the land and Abel became a sheepherder (Genesis 4: 2-3). After some time had passed, both Cain and Abel were led to offer oblations unto the Lord (Genesis 4: 3-4). Abel offered *meat* from his flock and Cain offered *fruit* from his field.

[4] *And Abel, he also brought of the firstlings of his flock and of the fat thereof. And the LORD had respect unto Abel and to his offering:*
[5] *But unto Cain and to his offering he had not respect. And Cain was very wroth, and his countenance fell*   Genesis 4: 4-5

The offering that Abel made to God was accepted and that by Cain was rejected...... *Why?* We are not told why God was displeased with the oblation of Abel and displeased with that of Cain, but one difference is obvious. The offering made by Abel was an animal (blood) sacrifice, and the offering made by Cain was a vegetable (bloodless) sacrifice. We know from later biblical records that a blood sacrifice was used in many biblical covenants, and was the basis of the New Covenant. However, the account of Genesis 4 was thousands of years from the ministry of Christ. It is also recorded that the offering of Abel was one of *Firstfruits*. However, if this caused God to accept the offering of Abel over that of Cain, there is no indication in the holy scriptures. Perhaps we should look elsewhere.

It seems likely that Abel gave his offering in faith, but Cain did not. *Without faith it is impossible to please God* (Hebrews 11:6).

[3] *Through faith we understand that the worlds were framed by the word of God, so that things which are seen were not made of things which do appear.*
[4] *By faith Abel offered unto God a more excellent sacrifice than Cain, by which he obtained witness that he was righteous, God testifying of his gifts: and by it he being dead yet speaks*   Hebrews 11: 3-4

In any case, Cain disliked what God had done, and he took his Wrath out on his brother Abel.

[8] *And Cain talked with Abel his brother: and it came to pass, when they were in the field, that Cain rose up against Abel his brother, and slew him.*   Genesis 4:8

This is the first instance of God's Wrath outside of the Garden of Eden and it was against only one man (Cain). God is omnipotent and He knew what Cain had done. In an act of mercy and grace, God gave Cain a chance to confess his sin and repent.

And the LORD said unto Cain: Where is Abel thy brother? And he said, I know not: Am I my brother's keeper?   Genesis 4:9

When Cain slew his brother Abel, God immediately knew what had happened. God omnipotent and man cannot hide their sins from Him. He knows the actions and heart of all men.

And the LORD said unto Cain: Why art thou wroth? and why is thy countenance fallen?   Genesis 4:6

How foolish mortal man is to think that he can fool God and hide his sin(s). The Lord continued to give Cain a chance to repent and confess his sin.

If thou doest well, shalt thou not be accepted? and if thou doest not well, sin lieth at the door. And unto thee shall be his desire, and thou shalt rule over him
Genesis 4:7

Nothing has changed after almost 6000 years. Man continues to sin even today and denies God. Sin *lies at the door* and seeks to destroy and control the actions of man. God had enough of Cain and his lies.

And God said: What hast thou done? **The voice of thy brother's blood cries unto me from the ground.** Genesis 4:10

Cain had been judged and found wanting. The Wrath of God was about to fall upon Cain. For what Cain had done to his brother, his sentence was as follows.

(1) From that point on, when Cain tilled and planted the earth, it would not yield her crops (Genesis 4:12-a)
(2) Cain was condemned to roam the earth by himself with no family or friends (Genesis 4: 12b)

Cain had been a farmer, and because the earth would no longer yield its fruit and because no one would commune with him, he said:

My punishment is greater than I can bear Genesis 4:13

[14] *Behold, thou hast driven me out this day from the face of the earth; and from thy face shall I be hid: I shall be a fugitive and a vagabond in the earth; and it shall come to pass, that every one that finds me shall slay me.*
[15] *And the LORD said unto him, Therefore whosoever might want to slay Cain, vengeance shall be taken on him sevenfold. And the LORD set a mark upon Cain, lest any finding him should kill him* Genesis 4: 4-14

Although the Wrath of God might be final, The Grace of God is never-ending. Cain never repented and felt sorry for what he had done, he was only concerned for his own sinful life. There is no indication that Cain ever repented for deliberately murdering his brother Abel. In an act of amazing grace, God told Cain that he would protect him. Protect him from what? Cain pleaded with God: *every one that finds me shall slay me* (Genesis 4:14). This in extremely interesting request. Who is out there to kill Cain? Cain and Abel were the first two offspring of Adam and Eve….at least they were the 1st two recorded in the Holy Scriptures. This is a mystery not explained. *Whoever* was out there, the concern of Cain must have been legitimate. In an act of grace, God placed a *mark* upon Cain as a sign that he was under divine protection (Genesis 4:15).

Cain not only survived, but after a period of wandering in the wilderness by himself, he married a woman in the Land of Nod near the Garden of Eden. He evidently prospered and produced many sons and daughters (Genesis 4: 16-22). Cain died in the Land of Nod when he was 730 years old, about 715 years after he killed his brother Abel. The dual nature of God is clearly revealed in this story. God is a fair and just God, but rather than kill Cain for what he had done to Abel, He only banished him to the wilderness for an indefinite amount of time. When Cain complained about his sentence, God protected him from someone or something that was also in the wilderness.

God's Wrath Upon Mankind: *The Great Flood*

As things got spiritually worse and worse, God was through with tolerating the sins of man. Among sinful man, God found a man named *Noah*, along with his 3 sons Shem, Ham and Joseph and their 4 wives. Noah was called by God: *a righteous man* (Genesis 7:1). God told Noah that He was about to destroy all that He had made upon the earth except for Noah, his 3 son and their 4 wives (Genesis 6:18). Noah and his family along with the animals which populated the earth would be saved by an ark which Noah and his sons were told to build. God told Noah that He would destroy the earth with a great flood which would be caused by 40 days and 40 nights of torrential rain. Except for the ark and its inhabitants, nothing would survive this Great Flood.

But Noah found grace in the eyes of the LORD
Genesis 6:8

This must have been quite a shock to Noah and his family: *What was a flood*? Most biblical scholars agree that up until this time there had never been rain upon the earth. Biblical and ancient records indicate that there was a canopy of mist that covered the entire earth. This mist provided moisture for all the crops which were grown, and also shielded mankind from any external damage from the sun and ultraviolet rays. It was this protection that allowed man to live hundreds of years before death. We now encounter a difficult passage of scripture which was spoken by God.

And the LORD said: My spirit shall not always strive with man, for that he also is flesh: yet his days shall be a hundred- and twenty-years   Genesis 6:3

The exact meaning of this rather obscure scripture has been debated for years by many biblical commentators and scholars. The 1st possibility which some believe is that by Genesis 6:3 it took 120 years for Noah and his sons to build the ark. Noah had 3 sons (Genesis 6:10) at age 500 (triplets or within a short span of time), and he was 600 years old when the flood came (Genesis 5:32, Genesis 7:6). This is only 100 years. Of course, Noah could have started building the ark at age 480 by himself and his sons helped later. The 2nd possibility is that the Genesis account does not actually say that Noah *and* his 3 sons built the ark, but is unlikely that Noah could have accomplished such a feat by himself and it is unimaginable that anyone in that sinful generation would help him besides his three sons. This possibility acknowledges that God had reached His limit of ignoring the sinful and wicked ways of all people upon this earth except for Noah and his family (Genesis 6:13, 17). When Noah was only 480 years old, God pronounced judgment on mankind and prophesied that He would strive (overlook the state of man) no longer. The people would have 120 years to repent or the Wrath of God would fall upon them all. The 3rd possibility, and a popular interpretation, is that God would limit the length of life to 120 years after the current generation died. This is obviously not true since much later *after* the flood Abraham lived to be 175 years old (Genesis 25:7). It is best not to speculate exactly what Genesis 6:3 actually meant, but the 2nd possibility seems to be the best. If God gave then 120 years warning, it would not be the first time that He gave His people time to repent before releasing His wrath. Even in the New Testament, when Christ died in 30 AD, God gave his chosen people (Israel) 40 years to repent and turn around before He destroyed Herod's Temple with fire, and took all but the very young and old people into Roman captivity in 70 AD.

Noah did *all that God commanded him* (Genesis 6:22). Noah built the ark, and over a period of 7 days (Genesis 7: 1-4) he put 7 pair of all clean animals and 2 pair of all unclean animals into the ark. Noah also took his wife, his 3 son's wives and his sons (8 people in all) into the ark. God sealed them into the ark and it rained for 40 days and 40 nights. The deluge flooded the earth and killed every living human and every living thing which walked upon the earth (Genesis 7:4). After exactly one year, Noah and his family left the ark to begin a new dispensation and to repopulate the earth.

[11] In the six hundredth year of Noah's life, in the second month, the seventeenth day of the month, the same day were all the fountains of the great deep broken up, and the windows of heaven were opened.
[12] And the rain was upon the earth forty days and forty nights.
[13] In the selfsame day entered Noah, and Shem, and Ham, and Japheth, the sons of Noah, and Noah's wife, and the three wives of his sons with them, into the ark
Genesis 7: 11-13

After the flood destroyed every living creature on the earth except for Noah and his family, imagine how Noah felt every time that it started to rain. In the flesh, he must have trembled and hid from what might be another outpouring of God's Wrath with another great flood. God must have seen this, and in Genesis 8:18 and Genesis 9:9 the 1st use of the word *covenant* appeared in the Holy scriptures.

*But with thee will I establish my **covenant**; and thou shalt come into the ark, thou, and thy sons, and thy wife, and thy sons' wives with thee.*   Genesis 8:18

*And I, behold, I establish my **covenant** with you, and with your seed after you*
Genesis 9:9

The covenant which God made with Noah was *perpetual, unconditional* and *unilateral.*

[11] And I will establish my covenant with you; neither shall all flesh be cut off any more by the waters of a flood; neither shall there anymore be a flood to destroy the earth.
[12] And God said: This is the token of the covenant which I make between me and

you and every living creature that is with you, for perpetual generations
Genesis 9: 11-12

The Lord promised Noah that He would never again destroy the world with water. To confirm the Covenant, He set a *rainbow* in the sky every time it rained.

[13] *I do set my bow in the cloud, and it shall be for a token of a covenant between me and the earth.*
[14] *And it shall come to pass, when I bring a cloud over the earth, that the bow shall be seen in the cloud:*

[15] *And I will remember my covenant, which is between me and you and every living creature of all flesh; and the waters shall no more become a flood to destroy all flesh.*
[16] *And the bow shall be in the cloud; and I will look upon it, that I may remember the everlasting covenant between God and every living creature of all flesh that is upon the earth.*
[17] *And God said unto Noah, This is the token of the covenant, which I have established between me and all flesh that is upon the earth*   Genesis 9: 13-17

And God blessed Noah and his sons, and said unto them: Be fruitful, and multiply, and replenish the earth   Genesis 9:1

[11] *And I will establish my covenant with you; neither shall all flesh be cut off any more by the waters of a flood; neither shall there anymore be a flood to destroy the earth.*
[12] *And God said, This is the token of the covenant which I make between me and you and every living creature that is with you, for perpetual generations:*
[13] *I do set my bow in the cloud, and it shall be for a token of a covenant between me and the earth.*
[14] *And it shall come to pass, when I bring a cloud over the earth, that the bow shall be seen in the cloud:*
[15] *And I will remember my covenant, which is between me and you and every living creature of all flesh; and the waters shall no more become a flood to destroy all flesh*   Genesis 9: 11-15

The Great Flood of Noah is not called the *Wrath of God* against mankind anywhere in the Biblical accounts of the flood, but it is difficult to call it anything else.

For the wrath of God is revealed from heaven against all ungodliness and unrighteousness of men, who hold the truth in unrighteousness   Romans 1:18

If God's Wrath does not explain the Great Flood…. What does?

The Dispensation of Man's Rule

After the Great Flood, Noah and his 3 sons began to repopulate the earth. This was the *Dispensation of Man's Rule*. Every man, woman and child that lives on the earth today came from the seed of Adam. Since Noah came from the seed of Adam, he possessed the old sin nature and was well aware of the difference between good and evil. The genealogy of Noah is shown below. Noah had 3 sons (Shem, Japheth and Ham) before the Great flood.

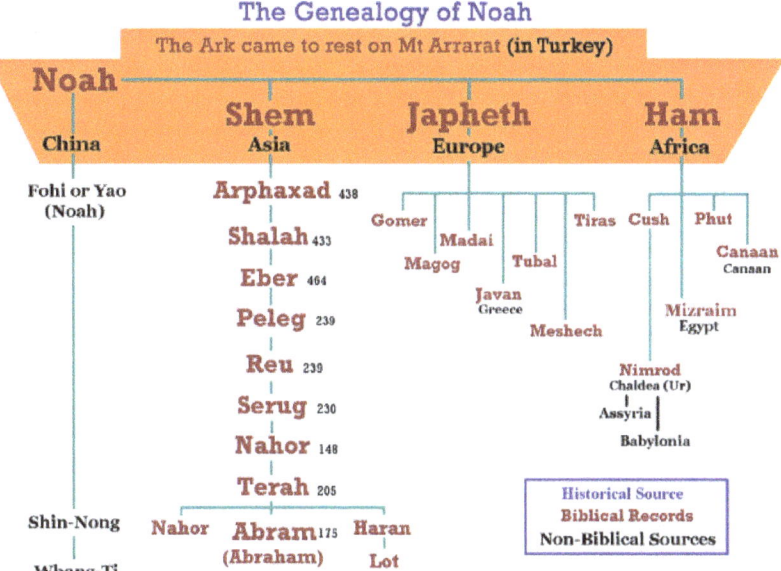

Nimrod and the City of Babel
After the flood, Ham had a son called Cush, and Cush begat *Nimrod*. Nimrod became a king in the land of Shinar, which was the southern part of Mesopotamia. Nimrod was described as a *mighty hunter*. It is not found in the Holy scriptures, but ancient records tell that Nimrod founded the *City of Babel*.
The *Tower of Babel* is described in Genesis 11.

[1] And the whole earth was of one language, and of one speech.
[2] And it came to pass, as they journeyed from the east, that they found a plain in the land of Shinar; and they dwelt there.
[3] And they said one to another: Go to, let us make brick, and burn them thoroughly. And they had brick for stone, and slime had they for mortar.
[4] And they said, Go to, let us build us a city and a tower, whose top may reach unto heaven; and let us make us a name, lest we be scattered abroad upon the face of the whole earth.
[5] And the LORD came down to see the city and the tower, which the children of men built.
[6] And the LORD said, Behold, the people is one, and they have all one language; and this they begin to do: and now nothing will be restrained from them, which they have imagined to do.
[7] Go to, let us go down, and there confound their language, that they may not understand one another's speech.
[8] So the LORD scattered them abroad from thence upon the face of all the earth: and they left off to build the city.
[9] Therefore is the name of it called Babel; because the LORD did there confound the language of all the earth: and from thence did the LORD scatter them abroad upon the face of all the earth.   Genesis 11: 1-9

Nimrod wanted to be like God, and he built a Great Ziggurat (Tower) that reached for the heavens. This displeased God, and in His Wrath, He destroyed the Tower of Babel. He then dispersed the people throughout the world and *confounded their language*.

The story of Babel explains why people were scattered, evolved across the entire world, and speak different languages. This story attests to the fact that Jehovah has always been a jealous God who cannot tolerate anyone who attempts to promote their own image and seeks to be worshipped above the living God. The story of Nimrod and Babel partially explains the concept of *evolution*, because men in different places throughout the world and in different climates would naturally change in physical appearance and adopt to the world around them. In any case, mankind **did not** evolve from apes and begin to walk upright as evolutionists would have us believe. However, there is no conflict regarding the fact that mankind has evolved into distinctly different human forms in different places…. this is self-evident. Regardless of how man evolved into different likenesses, the fact remains that the human anatomy and its various life-sustaining parts remain the same. Over thousands of years man changed his basic appearance and external composition naturally adapted to the environment in which they lived. Hence, people from Africa and South America are in outward appearance only different from those in Egypt or India.

Sodom and Gomorrah

The fundamental character and actions of man have not changed since Cain slew his brother Abel. Man is decidedly wicked and rebellious, and has been since Adam and Eve carried out the first sin. One of God's most destructive acts of Wrath against possibly the most sordid act in the entire Holy Bible was vividly demonstrated in the incident called *Sodom and Gomorrah*. Sodom and Gomorrah were twin cities which existed in the plains of Shinar. They are called *Cities of the Plain* (Genesis 13:12 and Genesis 19:29). The names of Sodom and Gomorrah have become synonymous with wicked and sinful people. Genesis 13:13 tells us that: *the*  *men of Sodom were wicked and sinners against the Lord*. Lot (who was the nephew of Abraham) lived there, and in Genesis 18 the Lord warned Abraham about how immoral both Sodom and Gomorra had become. He told Abraham that the twin-cities had become so corrupted that he would destroy them both. Abraham approached God and asked him: *Wilt thou also destroy the righteous with the wicked?* (Genesis 18:23). The Lord knew the answer all along, but He was further asked by Abraham: *If you can find 50 righteous people, will you destroy the Cities?* The Lord must have been amused, because He told Abraham: *I will do better that that, if I can find 45 righteous people, I will not pour my wrath out upon the city.* We are not told what happened next, but Abraham must have checked things out for himself; because he later approached God and asked him: *Will you hold your wrath if 40 people can be found?* God again agreed. This was repeated by Abraham for 30…then 20…then 10 righteous people. The answer was the same, and after the last inquiry the Lord tired of this game and left. As we read on, only Lot, his wife and his 2 daughters were righteous in both cities.

Shortly after, two angels of the Lord suddenly appeared at the house of Lot. After a short conversation, Lot agreed that they could spend the night in Lot's house. Before they could all retire, a large crowd of men from both cities appeared at Lot's door. The men spoke to Lot and told him to bring his guests outside with them so that they could have homosexual relations with them. In one  of the most bizarre responses in scripture, Lot had two virgin daughters and he offered them to the crowd instead of his guests! Upon hearing what Lot had offered, the angels pulled Lot back into the house and: *smote the men that were at the door of the house with blindness, both small and great* (Genesis 19:11). The story now becomes even more interesting. The angels which had visited Lot suddenly commanded him to gather his family because they had been sent there by God to destroy both Sodom and Gomorrah (Genesis 19:13). Lot had a total of 4 daughters in Sodom…two were married and two were not (virgins). Lot pleaded with his two married daughters and their husbands to leave the city, but they would not. So only Lot, his wife and his two unmarried daughters began to flee the city led by the angels.

Then the LORD rained upon Sodom and upon Gomorrah brimstone and fire from the LORD out of heaven   Genesis 19:24

As they left the burning city of Sodom, the angels told Lot and his family:

look not behind thee, *neither stay thou in all the plain; escape to the mountain, lest thou be consumed*   Genesis 19:17

But, the wife of Lot did not believe the angels and when she turned and looked back, she turned into a *pillar of salt*. There are several things which can be learned from this story.

1. The Lord will always protect and look after his people if they are faithful and believe

2.0 Any Christian who places his life at the feet of the Lord cannot have one foot in the world and one in heaven.

3.0 Flee from the bondage of sin and never look back.

4.0 Put your faith and trust in the Lord and not in things of this world.

5.0 Place your trust in *supernatural protection and in things which are not seen rather than things that are seen.*

6.0 One must trust God with *all your mind and all your heart.*

7.0 There is no such thing as being *half-saved or half-lost.* Believe upon the Lord your God with all your mind and all of your heart

As a new Covenant Christian, are you fully committed to Jesus Christ? Do you believe every word and every promise that was spoken by Jesus Christ?

The Dispensation of New Beginnings

As the end of the *Dispensation of Man's Rule* began to close, God did something which was to change the course of history. God wanted a people that He could call His own, and He was about to exercise His will. Adam had failed him in the Garden of Eden, and when he was expunged from the Garden and told to reproduce and populate the earth his progeny became so wicked that only Noah and 7 other members of his family were worth saving from a great flood. after the flood, Noah and his three sons were responsible for restoring mankind. Incredibly, as sons and daughters were born to Noah and his family, the people became sinful and rebellious. This moved God to initiate another plan for humanity that would serve Him and obey his commands. This time He would not destroy the earth and eradicate all sinful men and women, but He would choose a man of God to carry out His will and follow His commandments…… that man was called *Abram*. According to the biblical book of Genesis, Abram was a man of God who lived in *Ur of Chaldees*, which is part of what is known as *Mesopotamia*. When Abram was living in a place called Haran, God called him to found a new nation in an undesignated land that he later learned was *Canaan*. Abram was 70 years old when he was called by God. The Lord told him to leave Ur and go to place that He would show him. Abram took with him his wife Sari, his father, and Lot his brother's son: and they came unto a place called *Haran* and dwelt there. God promised Abram: *I will make of you a great nation, and I will bless you."* Abram was 75 years old when they finally left Ur of Chaldees. Abram was a man who played a large part in not only Israel and Judaism, but is still revered and is a part of Islam and Christianity today. Jews consider Abram to be the Father of Israel and Judaism.

Sarah and Abram were childless, but they were promised that they would birth from the seed of Abraham many nations and many kings. This covenant promise was made to Abraham when he was not much older than 75. By time Abraham was 86 years old he and Sarah both were in a state of disbelief. Sari approached Abram and came up with an incredibly bad idea. She asked Abram if he wanted to sleep with her handmaiden, *Hagar*. Instead of what he should have done as head of the household, Abram agreed. About nine months later, Hagar gave birth to *Ishmael*. This incestuous act by Abraham is what caused all of the problems that we see in the Middle East and Palestine today. Ishmael was not chosen by God to carry on the promised line of Abram, and his birth was a unilateral decision by Abram that was in direct opposition to what God had promised. Sari adopted Ishmael even though it was not her own biological offspring. This was the 1st act of disbelief against God. We will discover later that this was partly responsible for the *Wrath* that God unleashed on Israel in Egypt.

When Ishmael was 13 years old, God again visited Abram when he was age 90 years old. At that time, God initiated a new covenant with Abram called the *Abramic Covenant*.

God made a unilateral and unconditional covenant with Abram. It consisted of the following.

(1) The covenant which God made with Abram was only to him although it affected Sarah (Genesis 17:3)
(2) Abram and his wife Sarah would be fruitful and He would have many sons and daughters
(3) Abram would be the *Father of Many Nations* and kings (Genesis 17:6)
(4) Sarah his wife would be blessed and have many children (Genesis 17:16)
(5) Sarah his wife was 91 years old and Abram was 90 years old when God covenanted with Abram (Genesis 17:17)
(6) God assured them that they would bear a son, and that his name would be called *Isaac*

The Covenant which God established with Abraham was unconditional, but there would be 3 perpetual signs that would accompany God's promises: (1) Every male child that would be produced from the loins of Abram would be *circumcised.* (2) Abram's name would be changed from Abram which means *the father is exalted* to Abraham which in the Hebrew means *the father of many nations* (3) His wife Sarai whose name means *princess* would be changed to Sarah which means *noblewoman* in Hebrew. Abraham laughed at God when he was again promised a son (Genesis 17:17), but God assured Abraham that He would fulfill His *Covenant Promise.*

When Abraham was 99 years old and Sarah was 100, Sarah conceived and gave birth to the *Child of Promise* which was *Isaac*. The child which Abram had with the handmaiden of Sarah (Ishmael) was a product of incest and disbelief. Ishmael produced many children and grandchildren, but they were not the line of Abraham which God had promised him 25 years earlier. Isaac later married *Rebekah,* and that union produced a son called *Jacob* (Jacob means *Israel* in Hebrew). Jacob had 4 wives: Zilpah, Leah, Rachel and Bilhah. These 4 wives of Jacob eventually gave birth to the well-known 11 tribes of Israel (Zilpah…2 tribes, Leah….6 tribes, Rachel….1 tribe and Bilhah ….2 tribes).

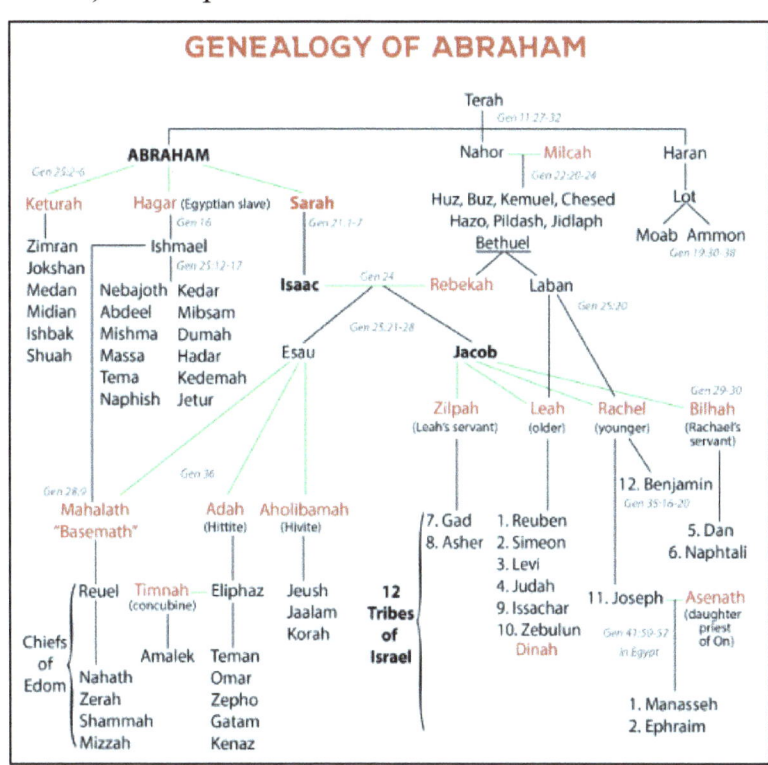

Jacob and one of his wives called *Rachel* produced a single son who we know as *Joseph* The astute reader will immediately recognize that this is only 11 future tribes. Joseph married an Egyptian priestess named *Asenath* and they had twin boys named *Manasseh and Ephraim*. In Genesis 47:28 and Genesis 48:22 as Jacob was about to die, he blessed Joseph's two sons Manasseh and Ephraim. The blessing that Jacob gave Joseph was that Joseph's two sons would become his sons. They became heir to the promise made to Jacob, and were both considered as part of the 12 Tribes of Israel.

It was not long until God tested the faith of Abraham once again. This time, Abraham passed the test. God told Abraham to take Isaac to one of the mountains in Moriah and offer him as a *burnt offering* to the Lord. Abraham did just that, and after he had prepared an altar of sacrifice and prepared to kill his son Isaac, the Lord stayed his hand and supplied a Ram in a burning bush instead. The response of Abraham to this command of God was what caused the apostle James to praise the *faith of Abraham*. (James 2: 22-24). Abraham believed that even if God had not stopped him from sacrificing his son Isaac, God would restore life to Isaac to preserve His Covenant Promise.

[17] *By faith Abraham, when he was tried, offered up Isaac: and he that had received the promises offered up his only begotten son,*
[18] *Of whom it was said: That in Isaac shall thy seed be called*
Hebrews 11: 17-18

It appropriate to type this act of God in supplying a ram to save Isaac, as a picture of God sending Jesus Christ as a substitute sacrifice for you and me. We are all sinners and not worthy of eternal life with Jesus Christ. But He provided payment for our sins, so that we can be stand before God as *justified* and sinless. God had promised Abraham: *And in thy seed shall all the nations of the earth be blessed; because thou hast obeyed my voice* (Genesis 22:18).

How could one man's children be responsible for the entire earth being blessed? The answer lies in the fact that one of Abraham's descendants would be the Savior of the world. Jesus was the fulfillment of this promise. The apostle Paul explains this clearly. *Now to Abraham and his seed were the promises made. He saith not, and to seeds, as of many; but as of one: And to thy seed, which is Christ* (Galatians 3:16). God's plan was at work the entire time; moving toward the sacrificial and atoning death of Jesus Christ.

Sometime after Abraham had died, Isaac and the decedents of Abraham were in the midst of a great 7-year famine which had struck the land of Canaan (Genesis 26:1). This was the 3rd such famine that Abraham had encountered since he was called into the Land of Canaan. Of the three, this one was by far the worse. It had not rained in 3 years and both livestock and people were dying. So, Jacob his 11 sons and 70 people in all packed up their belongings and moved to Egypt. The famine was a test from God, and the people failed.

What Was Israel Doing in Egypt?

There is no question concerning the fact that Israel as a nation spent 215 years in Egypt, and ultimately found themselves as slaves to the Pharaoh making bricks, mortar and cutting stones for great temples and pyramids. This is a historical and biblical fact. Several questions need to be investigated and answered is: *What were they doing there in the first place? Why was it necessary for the children of Israel to go into exile in Egypt and suffer oppression and slavery? What prevented their immediate inheritance of the land of Canaan, as promised by God to the patriarch Abraham?*

There should be little doubt that the sojourn of Israel and the plight in which they found themselves during this period of time was a result of *God's Wrath* upon the nation of Israel. God had promised Abraham:

[2] *I will make of thee a great nation, and I will bless thee, and make thy name great; and thou shalt be a blessing:*
[3] *And I will bless them that bless thee, and curse him that curses you: and in you shall all families of the earth be blessed.*   Genesis 12: 2-3

[15] *For all the land which thou seest, to thee will I give it, and to thy seed forever.*
[16] *And I will make thy seed as the dust of the earth: so that if a man can number the dust of the earth, then shall thy seed also be numbered.*
[17] *Arise, walk through the land in the length of it and in the breadth of it; for I will give it unto thee*   Genesis 13: 15-17

This is hardly what happened to the nation of Israel after they moved to Egypt. The 1st mention of Israel in Egypt is in Genesis 15.

[13] *And he said unto Abram: Know of a surety that thy seed shall be a stranger in a land that is not theirs, and shall serve them; and they shall afflict them four hundred years;*
[14] *And also that nation, whom they shall serve, will I judge: and afterward shall they come out with great substance.*

Egyptian Mural of Slaves Making Bricks

[16] *But in the fourth generation they shall come hither again: for the iniquity of the Amorites is not yet full*   Genesis 15: 13-14, 16

The Amorites were people who inhabited the land of Canaan when Abraham moved there from Ur. described in Genesis as descendants of Canaan, the son of Ham, (Genesis. 10:16).

The Amorites sinned so much that they defiled the land and proved themselves no longer worthy to live upon it (Leviticus 18:24-27; Deuteronomy 9:4-5; Amos 2:9; 1 Kings 14:24). We know God was merciful, giving them more than four centuries to show a change of heart, and He said that: *the iniquity of the Amorite is not yet complete,* So, Israel's deliverance would not come until the sin of the Amorites was *complete*. God is merciful, but God is also righteous. Wicked, sinful behavior has consequences.

One reason that Abraham did not immediately receive the blessings promised him by God is that the Amorites had not yet sinned against God to the point that their land would be taken away from them. *Would this explain why Israel spent many years of slavery and servitude in Egypt?* It might explain why the Israelites could not immediately inherit the land of Israel and had to temporarily sojourn in Egypt, but it does not explain why the Israelites chose to stay in Egypt. We need to look elsewhere.

Historically, God had always released His Wrath upon mankind because man had sinned and disobeyed His commandments. Israel had moved to Egypt because of a great 7-year famine. As part of Gods eternal plan, several years earlier Joseph, the youngest son of Abraham, had been sold into slavery in an act of jealousy by his brothers. Joseph was divinely taken to Egypt, and because of his ability to interpret visions and dreams he was appointed head of all of the grain and produce in Egypt. When Jacob and his other brothers came to Egypt, they did not know that God had placed Joseph there to help his family and other Israelites. Joseph made sure that his brothers and other descendants of Abraham were given choice parcels of land to live on and grain to sustain them. Israel multiplied and grew until the Pharoah began to worry that they might take over Egypt. It was then that Pharaoh decided to enslave Israel while he could do so. Again: *Why did God allow Israel to sink into servitude?*

According to the Jewish Rabbi David Kimchi (1160 AD-1235 AD), Israel was enslaved in Egypt as a result of *sin*. Their oppression was not a coincidental historical occurrence, but rather a divine punishment for wrongdoing. *What was the sin which incurred the harsh retribution of slavery and oppression?*

Jewish Rabbis offer three explanations for the slavery of Israel in Egypt.

(1) There was a Jewish Rabbi named *Shmuel* (1400 BC – 1060 BC) who was raised by a high priest named *Eli*. He was of the opinion that the sin for which the Israelites were enslaved in Egypt was Abraham's lack of faith in God. Abraham responded to God's promise of bequeathing him and his seed the Land of Canaan by asking: *By what shall I know that I shall inherit it?* (Genesis 15:8). He was not satisfied with God's promises, and so he requested a guarantee or a sign to believe God. Abraham's lack of faith in God's word resulted in the punishment and oppression of his offspring in Egypt.

(2) A Second opinion on why Israel was punished by God and wound up in Egyptian slavery came from Rabbi Moshe ben Nachman (1194 AD-127 AD). He was also of the opinion that Abraham's actions led to the enslavement in Egypt. However, he identified a different sin by Abraham. Rabbi Nachman was of the opinion that Abraham violated his covenant with God and demonstrated a lack of faith when he left Canaan and settled in Egypt during the second 7-year drought. By leaving the land of Canaan that he was given to live in by God (Genesis 12: 1-2), he demonstrated a complete lack of faith that God would not allow Abraham and his progeny to die in the Land of Canaan. It was because of this lack of faith, that exile and servitude in Egypt was decreed upon his children. It is somewhat paradoxical, but Abraham himself never experienced the Wrath of God in Egypt. Abraham lived to be 175 years old (Genesis 25:7) and he was buried by his two sons Isaac and Ishmael. God had made a promise to Abraham that: *thou shalt go to thy fathers in peace; thou shalt be buried in a good old age* (Genesis 15:15). God later declared that the sins of the fathers would fall upon: *the children's children, unto the third and to the fourth generation* (Exodus 34:7).

(3) Don Isaac Abrabanel (1437 AD-1508 AD) was a Rabbi who lived in Spain. He challenged the previous two reasons for the extended Egyptian slavery. Abrabanel suggested that rather than blame Abraham…. a man who was the father of Israel and revered for his great faith…. The people *chose* to remain

in Egypt and turned aside from God when they arrived in Egypt. In doing so, they brought pain and suffering upon themselves.

The scriptures indicate that when Jacob decided to lead the people to Egypt it was not just to obtain food and return during the 7-year famine, but he intended to stay there. When the people arrived, they were divinely protected by Joseph who had been sold into Egyptian slavery as a young man. Because he was able to interpret the dreams and visions of a Pharaoh, he was placed into a position of unusual influence and authority. He became guardian and custodian of all the grain in Egypt. He eventually arranged for the people to be given land in a fertile area called *Goshen* which Joseph set aside for them. Once Israel had settled in Goshen, the land and their position with Joseph was so good that they did not want to leave and return to the land of Canaan that God had promised to them. With food in their bellies and fertile land under their feet, why should they return to the land of Canaan?

Upon settling in their new land, the Israelites began to abandon their Jewish heritage. They wanted to obscure any behavior and appearance of their being different from the Egyptians. They did not circumcise their male children. In addition, they adopted to the sophisticated culture of the pagan Egyptians…. enthusiastically attending Egyptian cultural events and adopting to their modes of entertainment. Egyptian sports and theater were popular pastimes for the new foreign immigrants. The results proved to be disastrous, and rather than be a beacon of light to God and his mercy, they became disciples of darkness.

The people of Israel were assimilated into pagan Egyptian culture, which probably amused the warrior- like people of Egypt. The Egyptians had hundreds of pagan gods, and they would not accept one sovereign god, so it is not beyond reasoning that the Israelites would not publicly display their relationship to Jehovah. In addition, The Israeli women were beautiful and desired by the Egyptians, and the women of Israel were quick to seize the opportunity for wealth, position and social status as the wives or concubines of Egyptian royalty. This was a direct and sinful act of disobedience against God, who had forbidden marriage and relations with pagan males.

It is the author's belief that all of this is exactly what caused Israel to eventually fall into servitude and common laborers. As time passed, God allowed them to sink lower and lower into rebellion against his holy commands. Then in an act of tremendous love and grace, God heard their pleas to liberate them from Egyptian bondage. He started His plan by saving a unique Hebrew child.

Moses is Chosen by God

The Hebrews grew in number at an alarming rate. All of this did not go unnoticed, and eventually the Pharaoh began to fear them as at threat to Egyptian superiority. At this point he began to force both the men and women into virtual slaves. They were all relegated to making mortar and bricks for the gigantic temples and pyramids of Egypt (Exodus 1: 1-14). In order to eliminate the threat of a growing Israeli community, the Pharoah commanded that all male children born to a Hebrew woman would be cast into the River Jordan and drowned (Exodus 12:2). It is the author's belief that all of this was in God's plan and is exactly what caused Israel to eventually fall into servitude and common laborers. As time passed, God allowed them to sink lower and lower into rebellion against his holy commands. Then in an act of tremendous love and grace, God heard their pleas to liberate them from Egyptian bondage. He started His plan by saving a unique Hebrew child.

[1] And there went a man of the house of Levi, and took to wife a daughter of Levi.
[2] And the woman conceived, and bare a son: and when she saw him that he was a goodly child, she hid him three months.
[3] And when she could no longer hide him, she took for him an ark of bulrushes, and daubed it with slime and with pitch, and put the child therein; and she laid it in the flags by the river's brink.
[4] And his sister stood afar off, to decide what could be done for him.
[5] And the daughter of Pharaoh came down to wash herself at the river; and her maidens walked along by the river's side; and when she saw the ark among the flags, she sent her maid to fetch it.
[6] And when she had opened it, she saw the child: and, behold, the babe wept. And she had compassion on him, and said: This is one of the Hebrews' children.
[7] Then said his sister to Pharaoh's daughter, Shall I go and call to thee a nurse of the Hebrew women, that she may nurse the child for thee?
[8] And Pharaoh's daughter said to her, Go. And the maid went and called the child's mother.
[9] And Pharaoh's daughter said unto her: Take this child away, and nurse it for me, and I will give thee thy wages. And the woman took the child, and nursed it.
*[10] And the child grew, and she brought him unto Pharaoh's daughter, and he became her son. And she called his name **Moses**: and she said, Because I drew him out of the water*   Genesis 2: 1-10

Guided by nothing less than a divine act of God, the Pharaohs wife who adopted Moses went and chose without realizing it the actual mother of Moses to raise the child! And so, Moses grew up in the Pharaoh's palace with his real mother. He was a man of obvious mental and physical strength, and in God's own time he must have been told that he was not an Egyptian but a Hebrew. One day he was in the field and he saw an Egyptian man beating another Hebrew man to near death. Moses reacted by saving his Hebrew brother and killing the Egyptian.

Confused and fearing for his life, he left Egypt at age 40 and journeyed to the *Land of Midian* where he worked another 40 years as a sheep herder for a man called Jethro. After 80 years, God was ready to use Moses as His chosen vessel to liberate the Children of Israel who were still suffering in Egypt.

[23] And it came to pass in the passage of time, that the king of Egypt died: and the children of Israel sighed by reason of the bondage, and they cried, and their cry came up unto God by reason of the bondage.
[24] And God heard their groaning, and God remembered his covenant with Abraham, with Isaac, and with Jacob   Exodus 2: 23-24

[9] Now therefore, behold, the cry of the children of Israel is come unto me: and I have also seen the oppression wherewith the Egyptians oppress them.
[10] Come now therefore, and I will send thee unto Pharaoh, that thou mayest bring forth my people the children of Israel out of Egypt   Exodus 3: 9-10

Moses evidently stuttered, and because of this speech impediment God chose a Levite named Aaron to go with Moses. It had been a total of 430 years since God called Abraham to birth a new nation that would serve him. Israel had spent 215 years in the Land of Canaan and 215 years in the Egypt. This can be determined by carefully studying the Holy Scriptures.

The Hebrews grew in number and rank at an alarming rate. All of this did not go unnoticed, and eventually the Pharaoh began to fear them as at threat to Egyptian superiority. At this point he began to force both the men and women into virtual slaves. They were all relegated to making mortar and bricks for the gigantic temples and pyramids of Egypt (Exodus 1: 1-14). In order to eliminate the threat of a growing Israeli community, the Pharoah commanded that all male children born to a Hebrew woman would be cast into the River Nile and drowned (Exodus 12:2). It was in the midst of this onslaught that a Hebrew child who would be called *Moses* arose to serve God.

[1] And there went a man of the house of Levi, and took to wife a daughter of Levi.
[2] And the woman conceived, and bare a son: and when she saw him that he was

a goodly child, she hid him three months.
[3] And when she could no longer hide him, she took for him an ark of bulrushes, and daubed it with slime and with pitch, and put the child therein; and she laid it in the flags by the river's brink.
[4] And his sister stood afar off, to decide what could be done for him.
[5] And the daughter of Pharaoh came down to wash herself at the river; and her maidens walked along by the river's side; and when she saw the ark among the flags, she sent her maid to fetch it.
[6] And when she had opened it, she saw the child: and, behold, the babe wept. And she had compassion on him, and said: This is one of the Hebrews' children.
[7] Then said his sister to Pharaoh's daughter, Shall I go and call to thee a nurse of the Hebrew women, that she may nurse the child for thee?
[8] And Pharaoh's daughter said to her, Go. And the maid went and called the child's mother.
[9] And Pharaoh's daughter said unto her: Take this child away, and nurse it for me, and I will give thee thy wages. And the woman took the child, and nursed it.
[10] And the child grew, and she brought him unto Pharaoh's daughter, and he became her son. And she called his name **Moses***: and she said, Because I drew him out of the water*   Genesis 2: 1-10

Guided by nothing less than a divine act of God, the Pharaohs wife who adopted Moses went and chose without realizing it the actual mother of Moses to raise the child! And so, Moses grew up in the Pharaoh's palace with his real mother. He was a man of obvious mental and physical strength, and in God's own time he must have been told that he was not an Egyptian but a Hebrew. One day he was observing the Hebrews working, and he saw an Egyptian man beating a Hebrew man to near death. Moses reacted by saving his Hebrew brother and killing the Egyptian. Confused and fearing for his life, he left Egypt at age 40 and journeyed to the Land of Midian where he worked another 40 years as a sheep herder for a man called *Jethro*. After 80 years, God was ready to use Moses as His chosen vessel to liberate the Children of Israel who were still suffering in Egypt.

[23] And it came to pass in process of time, that the king of Egypt died: and the children of Israel sighed by reason of the bondage, and they cried, and their cry came up unto God by reason of the bondage.
[24] And God heard their groaning, and God remembered his covenant with Abraham, with Isaac, and with Jacob   Exodus 2: 23-24

[9] Now therefore, behold, the cry of the children of Israel is come unto me: and I have also seen the oppression wherewith the Egyptians oppress them.
[10] Come now therefore, and I will send thee unto Pharaoh, that thou mayest bring forth my people the children of Israel out of Egypt   Exodus 3: 9-10

[40] Now the sojourning of the children of Israel, who dwelt in Egypt, was four hundred and thirty years.
[41] And it came to pass at the end of the four hundred and thirty years, even the selfsame day it came to pass, that all the hosts of the LORD went out from the land of Egypt   Exodus 12: 40-41

The length of time that Israel spent in Egypt serving the Pharoah as essentially slaves has been the subject of much debate. Biblical literature contains estimates of 205 years, 215 years, 220 years and even 430 years. Why this is such a hotly debated topic is somewhat a mystery to this author. The Book of Genesis contains enough information to establish without any doubt that the Israelites spent exactly 215 years in Egypt and 215 years before that in the Land of Canaan. The following diagram is conclusive and can be verified.

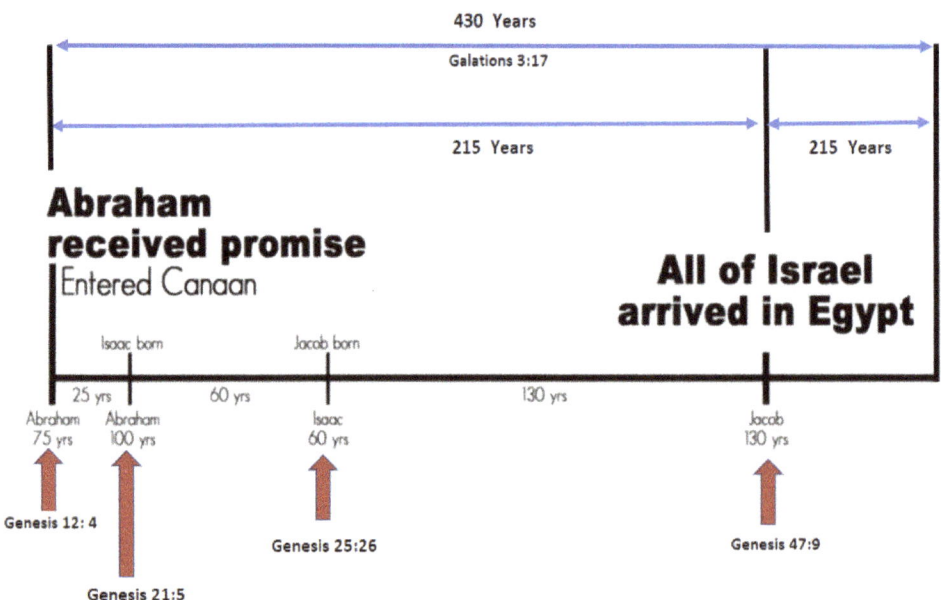

The Israelites had endured the Wrath of God for almost 215 years in Egypt in Egypt, although it was largely their fault. They finally realized that if they had just obeyed God and trusted Him in the Land of Canaan, that they would not be mired in the misery and suffering in which they found themselves. God had been watching and waiting for Israel to come to Him again. After years of serving the

Pharoah as slaves, the misery and affliction of making cutting stones and making bricks was more than the children of Israel could bear. They humbled themselves before the Lord and called upon Him for mercy.

[23] *And it came to pass in process of time, that the king of Egypt died: and the children of Israel sighed by reason of the bondage, and they cried, and their cry came up unto God by reason of the bondage.*
[24] *And God heard their groaning, and God remembered his covenant with Abraham, with Isaac, and with Jacob*   Exodus 3: 23-24

*In a little wrath I hid my face from thee for a moment; but with **everlast**ing kindness will I have mercy on thee*   Isaiah 54:8

God heard their cries and He chose Moses to set them free. The methods which were used by God represent the Wrath of God falling upon Egypt and the Pharoah through His servant Moses. There were two different points in time that the Wrath of God was made manifest: (1) Liberating Israel from Egyptian slavery (2) Rescuing Israel from the fury and vengeance of the Pharoah at the Red Sea.

Liberating Israel from Egyptian Slavery

The Israelites had endured the Wrath of God for 215 years in Egypt, and they finally realized that if they had just obeyed God and trusted in Him, that they would not be in the misery and suffering in which they found themselves. God had been watching and waiting for all those years for Israel to come to Him again. Finally, the Israelites turned to God and prayed for their deliverance. Isn't it strange that men and women often turn to God when anything else might be hopeless?

God heard their cries and Moses was chosen to rescue His people from Egyptian slavery. Moses would use miraculous and unimaginable methods to liberate the Israelites which can only be attributed to the Wrath of God falling upon Egypt and the Pharoah. There were two different points in time that the Wrath of God was made manifest: (1) Liberating Israel from Egyptian slavery (2) Rescuing Israel from the fury and vengeance of the Pharoah

God would hear the pleas of His people and send Moses and Aaron to the Pharoah to liberate the Nation of Israel from Egyptian slavery. He would cause the Pharoah to *let my people go* by causing 10 supernatural plagues to fall upon the people of Egypt.

The first plague was to turn the waters of the Nile River to blood. This must have caused millions of fish to die in the river, and the water was unusable. Pharaoh was told: *By this you will know that I am the LORD* (Exodus 7:17). But the Pharoah's heart was only hardened and he told Moses: *I will not let your people go.*

The second plague brought thousands of frogs from the Nile River, and these frogs invaded every Egyptian home. The frogs died and their rotting bodies were piled everywhere throughout the land. But the Pharoah's heart was only hardened and he told Moses: *I will not let your people go.*

The third plague was millions of gnats. They were everywhere, and the magicians were unable to duplicate this third plague: They declared to the Pharaoh: *This is the finger of God* (Exodus 8:19).

The fourth plague was flies which descended upon the entire land of Egypt. However, the Wrath of God miraculously did not fall upon the Israelites, only the Egyptians (Exodus 8:21–24). But the Pharoah's heart was only hardened and he told Moses: *I will not let your people go.*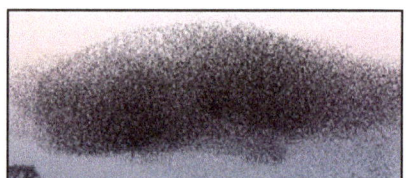

The fifth plague was the death of livestock. As with the previous plague, God protected His people from the plague, while the cattle of the Egyptians died. God was steadily destroying the economy of Egypt, while showing His ability to protect and provide for those who obeyed Him. (Exodus 9:7). The Result: Pharoah's heart was only hardened and he told Moses: *I will not let your people go.*

The sixth plague was boils upon the people of Egypt which were so severe that the magicians of Egypt could not stand before Moses. The Result: Pharoah's heart was only hardened and he told Moses: *I will not let your people go.*

Before God sent the last four plagues upon Egypt, the Pharaoh was given a special message from God. These plagues would be more severe than the others, and they were designed to convince Pharaoh and all the people: *that there is none like me in all the earth* (Exodus 9:14). Pharaoh was even told that he had become Pharoah by the power of God, so that He could show His power and declare that He was the one true God, and that all of the hundreds of Egyptian gods were only false gods.

As an example of His grace, God warned Pharoah to gather whatever cattle and crops remained from the previous plagues and shelter them from the coming storm. Some of Pharoah's servants heeded the warning (Exodus 9:20), while others did not.

The seventh plague was hail throughout all the land. The hail destroyed all of the wheat and barley which was so important to the Egyptians. This hail was unlike any that had been seen before. It was accompanied by a fire which grew in the ground was devastated by the hail and fire.
Again, the children of Israel were miraculously protected, and no hail damaged anything in their lands. Once again: Pharoah's heart was only hardened and he told Moses: *I will not let your people go.*

Before God brought the 8th plague, He told Moses that the Israelites would be able to tell their children of the things they had seen God do in Egypt and how it demonstrated His unlimited power. *The eighth plague* was swarms of locusts.

Any crops which had not been destroyed by hail, were now devoured by the swarms of locusts. There would be no harvest in Egypt that year. But Pharoah's heart was only hardened and he told Moses: *I will not let your people go.*

 *The ninth plague* was darkness which fell upon all of Egypt for three days. To demonstrate his power over daylight and darkness, the homes of the Israelites had light. Sadly: Pharoah's heart was only hardened and he told Moses: *I will not let your people go.*

The Tenth Plague: The stage was set for the last plague to fall upon Pharoah and the people of Egypt. The tenth and last plague was the *death of all firstborn males* of animals and all who lived in Egypt. Unlike the other plagues, which the Israelites survived by virtue of their identity as God's people, this plague required an act of faith by each Israeli household. God commanded each family to take an unblemished male lamb and kill it. The blood of the lamb was to be smeared on the top and sides of their doorways, and the lamb was to be roasted and eaten that same night. Any family that did not follow God's instructions would suffer both their firstborn child and the firstborn of their animals to be killed. The instrument of God's Wrath would be a destroying angel which God would send throughout the land. This angel was told to destroy all the

firstborn throughout the land of Egypt, whether human or animal. The only protection was the blood of the lamb on the door. When the destroyer saw the blood, he would pass over that house and leave it untouched (Exodus 12:23). *The Feast of Passover* is a Jewish Festival still held today in remembrance of this tragic event. Passover is a memorial of that night in ancient Egypt when God delivered His people from bondage. But Passover also foreshadowed our Savior Jesus Christ. Paul in I Corinthians 5:7 teaches that Jesus became our Passover when He died to deliver us from the bondage of sin. While the Israelites who obeyed God and smeared the blood of a lamb on the lintel of each door were spared, every other home in the land of Egypt experienced God's Wrath as their first-born were killed by the angel of death.

During this night which was a night to be much remembered, the Pharoah of Egypt did not escape the Wrath of God and his firstborn son was killed during the evening hours. This happened on Thursday night, Nisan 15. God had finally moved the Pharoah to declare: *Go.... Get out of Egypt.* On the morning of Thursday, Nisan 15, the Children of Israel left Israel led by Moses and Aaron.

The Wrath of God: *Red Sea Crossing*

Pharoah mourned the death of his only child for 3 days, and then he *hardened his heart* again. In a fit of rage, he assembled all of his chariots and his soldiers and pursued Moses and the Children of Israel across the Sinai Peninsula. Pursuing over a million men, women and children: it did not take him long to catch up to the fleeing multitude. He caught up with Moses in the southern reach of the Sinai Peninsula as they camped beside an arm of the Red Sea called the *Gulf of Aquaba*.

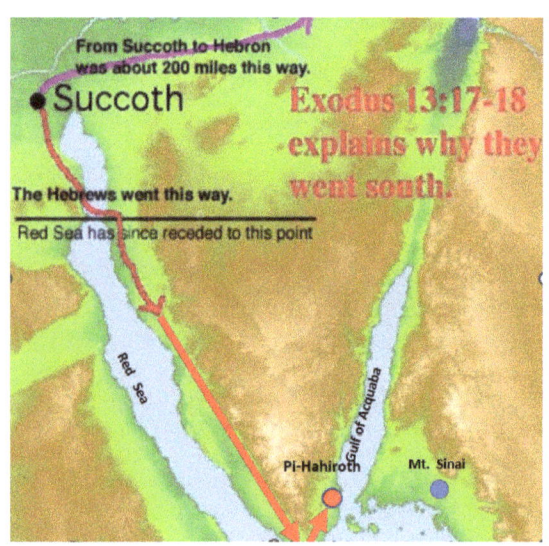

Moses was hemmed in by mountains to the north, a main body of the Red Sea to the west and south, and the Gulf of Aquaba to the south and west. But God rescued Israel once again.

[13] *And Moses said unto the people, Fear ye not, stand still, and see the salvation of the LORD, which he will shew to you today: for the Egyptians whom ye have seen today, ye shall see them again no more forever.*

[14] The LORD shall fight for you, and ye shall hold your peace.
[15] *And the LORD said unto Moses, Wherefore cry thou unto me? speak unto the children of Israel, that they go forward:*
[16] *But lift thou up thy rod, and stretch out thine hand over the sea, and divide it: and the children of Israel shall go on dry ground through the midst of the sea.*
Exodus 14: 13-16

When Moses lifted up his rod, the Red Sea (Gulf of Aquaba) parted and the waters raised up on two sides creating a path to the other side (Land of Midian). All of the people crossed the Red Sea on dry land as the Lord protected in from a cloud to the north.

[19] *And the angel of God, which went before the camp of Israel, removed and went behind them; and the pillar of the cloud went from before their face, and stood behind them:*
[20] *And it came between the camp of the Egyptians and the camp of Israel; and it was a cloud and darkness to them, but it gave light by night to these: so that the one came not near the other all the night.*
[21] *And Moses stretched out his hand over the sea; and the LORD caused the sea to go back by a strong east wind all that night, and made the sea dry land, and the waters were divided.*
[22] *And the children of Israel went into the midst of the sea upon the dry ground: and the waters were a wall unto them on their right hand, and on their left*
Exodus 14: 19-22

The Egyptian army was held at bay by the angel of the Lord until a strong east wind blew all night, caused the Red Sea (Gulf of Aquaba) to part, and dried the bottom until it was ready for passage. The Gulf of Aquaba was crossed on dry land by the Israelites on Sunday morning. They arose from the water on exactly the same day that Jesus Christ arose from the grave and conquered death.

The Egyptians were allowed to pursue Moses and the people. But, as they were crossing in hot pursuit, God removed the wheels from all their chariots so that they could not go back (Exodus 14:25). Suddenly the walls of water closed in upon them and they were all drowned. Thus, the Wrath of God once again fell upon the Egyptians and they were all destroyed (Exodus 14: 26-28).

The Children of Israel marched out of Egypt on Nisan 15, and after a 3-day journey they camped in the southern part of the Sinai Peninsula just north of the

Gulf of Aquaba which is part of the Red Sea. Moses camped at a place called Pi-Hahiroth which is west of Mt Sinai and the Land of Midian.

As Moses was approaching the campsite at Pi-Hahioth, the Egyptian Pharoah once against hardened his heart, and with an army of soldiers pursued the fleeing Israelites (Exodus 14: 1-8). With the Egyptian army closing fast from the north and the Red Sea to the south, Moses had no place to go. Moses cried to the Lord for mercy, and the Lord heard his cry.

While Moses looked on with his hands raised to heaven, God parted the Red Sea and the children of Israel crossed upon dry land until they were all safely across. As Israel watched from the Horeb, the armies of Pharoah pursued them and once they were all crossing the bottom of the Red Sea, God caused the water to return upon them from both sides and they were all drowned. Hence, God in His righteous anger once again saved the Children of Israel.

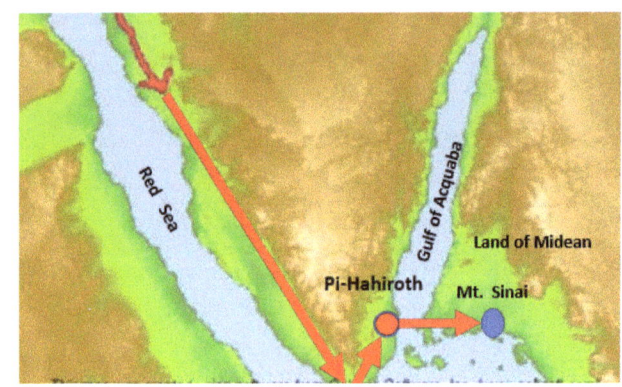

[26] *And the LORD said unto Moses, Stretch out thine hand over the sea, that the waters may come again upon the Egyptians, upon their chariots, and upon their horsemen.*
[27] *And Moses stretched forth his hand over the sea, and the sea returned to his strength when the morning appeared; and the Egyptians fled against it; and the LORD overthrew the Egyptians in the midst of the sea.*
[28] *And the waters returned, and covered the chariots, and the horsemen, and all the host of Pharaoh that came into the sea after them; there remained not so much as one of them.*
[29] *But the children of Israel walked upon dry land in the midst of the sea; and the waters were a wall unto them on their right hand, and on their left.*
[30] *Thus the LORD saved Israel that day out of the hand of the Egyptians; and Israel saw the Egyptians dead upon the sea shore.*
[31] *And Israel saw that great work which the LORD did upon the Egyptians: and the people feared the LORD, and believed the LORD, and his servant* Moses
Exodus 14: 26-31

Dispensation of the Law

After camping and celebrating East of the Red Sea (Gulf of Aquaba), Moses led them all to Mt. Sinai where they waited to receive God. All seemed well…. Israel had been saved from Pharoah and his army and after crossing the Red Sea they became an independent nation. God had given them Manna when they were hungry, and He had given them water when they were thirsty. The time had come for God to give them the 10 Commandments and 113 other laws by which they should live.

Moses and the Children of Israel took 47 days to reach Mt. Sinai since they had departed from Egypt. As soon as Moses reached Mt. Sinai, Moses ascended the mountain to meet with God. God spoke to Moses and revealed His plan for the Nation of Israel.

[5] Now therefore, if ye will obey my voice indeed, and keep my covenant, then ye shall be a peculiar treasure unto me above all people: for all the earth is mine: [6] And ye shall be unto me a kingdom of priests, and a holy nation. These are the words which thou shalt speak unto the children of Israel   Exodus 19: 5-6

Israel had been chosen as God's own people. He would set them aside from all other people on the earth, and they would be a *peculiar treasure* to Him alone. They would be a *Kingdom of Kings and Priests*.

[7] And Moses came and called for the elders of the people, and laid before their faces all these words which the LORD commanded him.
[8] And all the people answered together, and said: All that the LORD hath spoken we will do. And Moses returned the words of the people unto the LORD.
[9] And the LORD said unto Moses: Lo, I come unto thee in a thick cloud, that the people may hear when I speak with thee, and believe thee forever. And Moses told the words of the people unto the LORD.
[10] And the LORD said unto Moses: Go unto the people, and sanctify them today and tomorrow, and let them wash their clothes,
[11] And be ready against the third day: for the third day the LORD will come down in the sight of all the people upon mount Sinai.   Exodus 19: 7-11

Over a 3-day period of time, Moses would ascend and descend Mt Sinai a total of 8 times. On the 50th day He would ascend from Mt. Sinai, God would appear in a thick cloud and He would give them the 10 commandments. This is shown in the following table.

Trip			Duration	Purpose
		Moses Ascended Mt. Sinai 8 Times		
		Moses and Israel arrive at Mt Sinai after a 47 day journey from Egypt (Ex 19: 1-2) Mt. Sinai is about 7500 feet tall		
1	Ex 19:3	Moses *ascends* Mt. Sinai 1st Time	Short Time	God confirms *Covenant* with Israel (Ex 19:5): Israel will be Holy nation & Kingdom of Priests (Ex 19: 6)
	Ex 19:7	Moses *decends* Mt. Sinai 1st Time		Covenant presented to People: *All that the LORD hath spoken we will do* (Ex 19:8)
2	Ex 19:8	Moses *ascends* Mt. Sinai 2nd Time	Short Time	God gives Moses intructions for people to meet Him. He will speak from a dark cloud (Ex 19:9)
				People told to sanctify themselves for 2 days, and God will descend to speak on the 3rd day (Ex 19:11)
				Moses is to set bounds around mountain (Ex 19:12).
				Whosoever toucheth the mount shall be surely put to death (Ex 19:12)
	Ex 19:14	Moses *decends* Mt. Sinai 2nd Time		Moses returns. Tells the people to prepare for God on the 3rd day (Ex 19:15)
	Ex 19:15			On Morning of 3rd day, people gather to meet with God (Ex 19: 17)
				Lord ascends to Mt. in dark smoke; trumpet sounds (Ex 19:19)
3	Ex 19:20	Moses *ascends* Mt. Sinai 3rd Time	Short Time	God calls Moses up morning of 3rd day: Tells people not to come up on Sinai (Ex 19: 21-23)
	Ex 19:25	Moses *decends* Mt. Sinai 3rd Time		God instructs people on how to live and verbally gives the 10 Commandments (Ex 20: 1-17)
				People quake in fear: People send Moses near to God in darkness where He is speaking (Ex 20: 18-21)
4	Ex 20:21	Moses *ascends* Mt. Sinai 4th Time	Short Time	God Instructs Moses to build an altar for burnt and Peace offerings (Ex 20: 22-26)
				God gives verbal laws on how to worship and live to Moses (Ex 21: 1-33)
	Ex 24:3	Moses *decends* Mt. Sinai 4th Time		Moses builds altar of sacrifice: Accepts God's covenant with Israel by blood offering (Ex 24: 4-8)
5	Ex 24:9	Moses *ascends* Mt. Sinai 5th Time	Short time	Moses ascends with Aaron, Nadab, Abihu and seventy elders (Ex 24: 1-2, 24:9)...(Compare to Ex 24:14)
	(Deut 9:9)			All see God in some way or another, and Moses is told to come up further (Ex 24 :10-11)
	Ex 24:12	Moses *descends* Mt. Sinai 5th Time		Moses must descend after Gen 24:11, but this is not recorded between Gen 24:11 and Gen 24:12
				(Compare Gen 24:1 and Gen 24:9 to Gen 24 13)

On the morning of the 3rd day, God descended from Mt Sinai.

[16] *And it came to pass on the third day in the morning, that there were thunders and lightnings, and a thick cloud upon the mount, and the voice of the trumpet exceeding loud; so that all the people that was in the camp trembled.*
[17] *And Moses brought forth the people out of the camp to meet with God; and they stood at the nether part of the mount.*   Exodus 19: 16-17

God descended from Mt. Sinai in a cloud of dark smoke (Exodus 19:19). God then spoke to the people and verbally gave them the 10 commandments (Exodus 20: 1-17). This is the 3rd ascension and descension of Mt. Sinai by Moses. Moses is up and down Mt. Sinai two more times (See Table).

6	Ex 24:12	Moses *ascends* Mt sinai 6th Time	40 Days & 40 Nights	This time, only Joshua and Moses go up (Ex 24:13). Aaron, Hur and elders stay (Ex 24:14)
				Moses leaves Joshua and goes further up Mt. Sinai (Ex 24: 15)
				Cloud covers Moses for 6 days and nights... On 7th day Moses is called out of cloud (Ex 24:16)
				Moses stays for 40 days and 40 nights (Ex 24:18, Deut 9:18). He is given two tablets of stone (Ex 24:12, Deut 9:9), and then he is given instructions on how to build the Tabernacle, all of the furniture, and duties of the Levites (Ex 25-31)
				Aaron and the people sin, construct a Golden Calf to worship (Ex 32: 1-6)
				Moses is told of rebellion and commanded to return (Ex 32 : 7-9)
				Lord wants to drestroy all of the people in His Wrath (Ex 32: 8- 10).
				Moses pleads for the people and God calms himself (Ex 32: 11-14)
	Ex 32: 15-16	Moses *decends* Mt. Sinai 6th Time		Moses returns with Joshua (Ex 32: 17-18)
	(Deut 9:21)			Moses is so mad he breaks the 2 tablets God had written upon the ground (Ex 32:19, Deut 19:17)
				Moses destroys Golden calf (Ex 32: 20-25)
				He then called for repentence, and only the Levites respond (Ex 32:26).
				The tribe of Levi comes to Moses and kill 3000 men (Ex 32: 27-28).
				God sends a plague upon rest of people (Ex 32:35).
7	Ex 32:31	Moses *ascends* Mt. Sinai 7th Time	Short Time	Moses plead for sins of people (Ex 32: 32-33)
				The Lord wants to eradicate all of the people, but shows mercy (Ex 32: 34, Deut 9: 12-14)
	Ex 33:1	Moses *decends* Mt. Sinai 7th Time		Moses descends the Mountain: Told to lead the people to Land of Canaan (Ex 33: 1-6)
				Moses moves the Tabernacle away from the people (Ex 33: 7-12)
				.....but Moses needs further instuctions and asks the Lord to tell him more (Ex 33: 13-16)
				God instructs Moses to make two new tablets of stone, bring them to the Mt., and he will write the 10 Commandments again (Exodus 34: 1-2)

Moses ascends again for 6th time, and this time he spends 40 days and 40 nights on Mt. Sinai. God writes the 10 Commandments upon two tablets of stone and then he gives instructions on how to build the Tabernacle and how the Levitical priesthood should function. Near the end of 40 days, God reveals to Moses that a terrible thing has happened. When Moses ascended for the 6th time, he left Aaron in charge. If Moses could trust anyone, it would be Aaron the High Priest.

Aaron and the Golden Calf

Incredibly, the people were scared that Moses would not return, and approached Aaron to do something. Aaron took gold from all of the people and made a Golden Calf. The people then engaged in sordid and despicable debauchery, even removing their clothes and engaged in lewd sexual behavior. After 40 days Moses immediately returns with Joshua and the two tablets, and upon arriving he sees

Aaron and all the people in sinful and rebellious acts. Moses is so mad he throws the two tablets to the ground and breaks them into pieces. He then calls for all who would repent of their sins to come to him…. only the Levites came to Moses. The Levites then drew their swords and killed 3000 Israelites. The next morning, Moses told the remaining people that he would ascend Mt. Sinai a 7th time to plead for the people and to make atonement for their sins. Moses ascends the mountain a 7th time, and speaks to the Lord. God is so mad that He wants to kill *all* of the people. Moses …. In an effective and compelling argument…. talks to God and His wrath was calmed, but He vowed to erase the names of all who rebelled against Him out of His *Book of Life* (Revelation 20:15). God then tells Moses to prepare the people for a journey to the *Land of Canaan*.

Moses descends a 7th time, and he moves the *Tabernacle* to a place just outside of camp. Moses needs more instructions from God, and so God calls him to Mt. Sinai for and 8th and final time. Before leaving, God instructs Moses to carve two new tablets out of stone and bring them to Mt. Sinai.

8	Ex 34: 2-5	Moses *ascends* Mt. Sinai 8th Time	40 Days & 40 Nights	Moses carves two new tablets of stone, and takes them to God up on Mt. Sinai (Ex 34: 1,4)
				God once again writes the 10 commandments on the two stones (Ex 34:1, Deut 10:3)
				He then reinforces the covenant that He had made with Israel (Ex 34: 10-27).
				Moses spends 40 days and 40 nights on Mt. Sinai (Ex 34:28, Deut 10:10)
	Ex 34:29	Moses *decends* Mt. Sinai 8th Time		When Moses finally came down, His face shown brightly as if it were a great light (Ex 34:29)
				Moses covered His face except when he was talking with the Lord (Ex 24: 29-35).

Moses ascends the mountain an 8th time. God once again writes the 10 commandments on the two new tablets of stone. God then commands Moses to return and put them in the ark of the Covenant with a pot of manna and Aaron's rod that budded. God then reinforces the covenant that He had made with Abraham. Moses once again spends 40 days and 40 nights on Mt. Sinai with the Lord.

When Moses finally descended, his face shone so brightly from being in the prescence of God that Moses had to cover his face when speaking with the people. This was when Moses began his trek to the Land of Canaan with the people (For more detail, anyone interested should read Phillips; *The Exodus*). Incredibly, it would not be long until the Children of Israel once again began to complain and rebel against the Laws of God.

Nadab and Abihu
Nadab was a close friend, a defender of Moses and a son of Aaron (Exodus 6:23). He was chosen to accompany Moses on his 5th trip up Mt. Sinai (Exodus 28:1), and he was appointed by Moses to be a minister to the people. However, like all of the other Israelites (except Joshua and Caleb) he soon apostatized and willingly chose to not trust God. His story is a stern warning and a stark reminder of the consequences of disobeying God's commands in the Old Testament. It is also an object lesson of how Satan can turn strong Christians against the will of God in both the Old and New Testaments.

In Exodus 22-26 after Moses had ascended Mt. Sinai for the 4th time, God instructed Moses on how to build the Tabernacle and He gave instructions as to how the Levites were to serve Him and the people on a daily basis. These commands to Moses were no ordinary set of instructions. They were very detailed and the Levites were to exactly follow every command or suffer the consequences.

When the Lord wished to speak with Moses, He would come to Moses inside the Tabernacle. Only Moses was allowed to talk with God. God selected Aaron as the first High Priest, and then he appointed Nadab and Abihu to serve at the *Altar of Sacrifice* where the people would atone for their sins with sin offerings, peace offerings and trespass offerings. The Alter of Sacrifice was a special place where the blood of animals would be offered as atonement for sins, and the meat would either be completely consumed by fire as an offering to the Lord, cooked for the Priesthood or cooked for the people. A unique and peculiar feature of the Altar of sacrifice were the coals used to cook the animals. The fire in the altar was originally started by God, and it was never to go out (Leviticus

6: 12-13). A special container was used to transport the coals from one camp to another, and no *strange fire* (Leviticus 10:1) could be used at the altar (Leviticus 6:9). The exact meaning of Strange Fire is unknown, but it is generally regarded as "fire that was unauthorized by God". Every day coals from the old fire were used to start a new fire, and in this way the original fire that was started by God would remain unique and holy.

We can only imagine what happened to Abihu and Nadab on that fateful day. Perhaps they arrived one morning and finding the coals were burning out, added some wood from somewhere else in the tabernacle. Both Aaron and his firstborn sons were forbidden to drink but maybe they had both been partying all night and were not thinking clearly. Maybe they just thought they could get away with it…. who knows? In any case, they were using unauthorized or *strange fire*.

[1] *And Nadab and Abihu, the sons of Aaron, took either of them his censer, and put fire therein, and put incense thereon, and offered strange fire before the LORD, which he commanded them not.*
[2] *And there went out fire from the LORD, and devoured them, and they died before the* Leviticus 10: 1-2

In an outpouring of God's Wrath, both Nadab and Abihu were immediately consumed with fire from heaven and died. Both bodies and all of their priestly garments were carried outside the camp and burned (Leviticus 10: 3-9).

Why did God react so violently to this single transgression? This all happened almost immediately after the Tabernacle had been erected and the Levites began administering to all of the people. Nadab and Abihu blatantly disregarded God's commands, and they had been given clear and straightforward instructions as to how they would serve. If Nadab and Abihu's sin had been done through ignorance, they would have been told to bring a sin-offering. But we can infer that it was done deliberately and arrogantly, and in direct contempt of God's majesty and justice. They therefore paid the ultimate price for the *wages of sin is death*. The sin and punishment of these priests showed the imperfection of the priesthood from the very beginning.

Every Christian today struggles with sin, and Satan is constantly trying to destroy every Christian by every temptation imaginable. Every Christian will sin intentionally or un intentionally, but we are no longer condemned by it. All Christians are born-again into the body of Christ, and is a new creation (Romans 6:

1-2, Colossians 3: 9-10). Thank God who no longer sees us in sin, but when He looks at us now, He only sees His sinless Son.

As in so many cases, the new Nation of Israel saw what happened to Nadab and Abihu, and they witnessed the Wrath of God, but it was quickly ignored and forgotten. It was not long before God began to move the people towards the promised land, and one of their first campsites was a place called *Taberah*. Taberah was not a unique campsite, evidently the people complained constantly in spite of the fact that God gave the meat (quail) and bread (manna) every day. *And when the people complained, it displeased the LORD: and the LORD heard it; and his anger was kindled; and the fire of the LORD burnt among them, and consumed them that were in the uttermost parts of the camp* Numbers 11:1

No wonder God called them a *stiff-necked people* (Exodus 32:9).

The Exodus from Egypt started on the 1st day of the Feast of Firstfruits (Nisan 15) and after two years year Moses had led the Children of Israel to the Jordan River just south of the promised land. During these two years the people became a rebellious people.

Korah's Rebellion
Korah was a great-grandson of Levi and a first cousin to Moses and Aaron. He was a wealthy man who being a Levite was part of the tribe that assembled and reassembled the Tabernacle as it moved from place to place. Korah was jealous of Aaron his cousin who had been chosen by God to serve as High Priest. He assembled a group of 250 other men who also felt that Moses was assuming too much authority. These men had forgotten that Moses and Aaron were not in leadership positions by chance, but that both had been chosen and appointed by God. The truth is that Korah and those who joined him in challenging Moses were jealous and wanted more recognition and authority. They all confronted Moses and claimed that he had appointed his brother Aaron as High Priest on his own accord, without being instructed to do so by God. They further demanded that they all be allowed to serve as High Priests. Their complaints rapidly became the centerpiece of a full-blown rebellion. When Moses was accused of elevating himself above the other people, he wisely declared that the Lord would decide who should lead the people.

Korah and his 250 followers were instructed to take coals from the *Altar of Incense* and fill their censors. The Lord would choose those He wanted to lead the people…. Moses and Aaron or the group that had assembled to follow Korah. The next day the 250, Moses, Aaron and Korah all filled their censors with coals and incense and gathered around the door of the Tabernacle. As they stood there, God appeared and spoke.

[18] *And they took every man his censer, and put fire in them, and laid incense thereon, and stood in the door of the tabernacle of the congregation with Moses and Aaron.*
[19] *And Korah gathered all the congregation against them unto the door of the tabernacle of the congregation: and the glory of the LORD appeared unto all the congregation.*
[20] *And the LORD spoke unto Moses and unto Aaron, saying,*
[21] *Separate yourselves from among this congregation,* **that I may consume them** *in a moment.* Numbers 16: 18-21

Moses warned the rest of the people to stay clear of the tents of Korah, Dathan and Abiram and speaking to the crowd he foretold of the punishment that would befall them: *the earth would open its mouth and swallow them alive* (Numbers 16:30). Just as Moses finished addressing the congregation that had gathered there the *Wrath of God* fell upon many who had gathered there in spite of God's warning.

[32] *the earth opened her mouth, and swallowed them up, and their houses, and all the men that followed Korah, and all their worldly possessions.*
[33] *They, and all that followed after Korah, went down alive into the pit, and the earth closed upon them: and they perished from among the congregation.*
[34] *And all of Israel that were round about them fled at the cry of them: for they said, Lest the earth swallow us up also.* Numbers 16: 32-34

God then turned to the 250 who had filled their censors with coals and incense and consumed them with fire from heaven (Numbers 16:35). Before all the people could scatter from the prescence of the Lord, He commanded Moses and Aaron to turn aside so that He could destroy all the rebellious people. Moses instantly told Aaron to take a censor, fill it with coals and incense from the Altar of Incense, and run out amidst the people to turn away the Wrath of God. Aaron did as he was told, but before he could appease the Lord, God had destroyed 14,700 people with a plague.

To further confirm and demonstrate that the authority of Moses and Aaron was by divine appointment, *each* member of the 12 tribes of Israel were commanded to choose a rod/staff, and inscribe their name upon it. The *tribe of Levi* would choose only one staff and the name of Aaron would be written upon it. The Lord would choose a single rod and that person would be *High Priest* (Numbers 17:5). Moses put all of the rods inside the Tabernacle, and the next day God commanded Moses to inspect all of the rods.

Moses went into the tabernacle of witness; and, behold, the rod of Aaron for the house of Levi was budded, and brought forth buds, and bloomed blossoms, and yielded almonds. Numbers 17:8

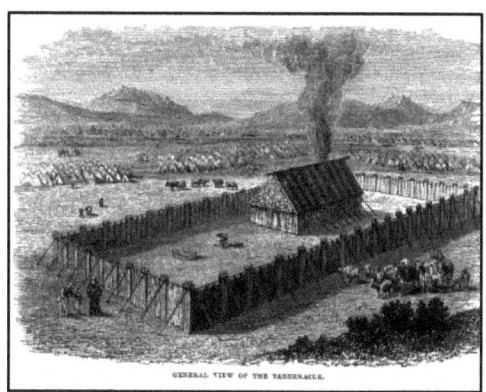

The Lord then spoke to Aaron and anointed him as High Priest. He and his sons and their sons would serve the people of Israel inside the Tabernacle and assist Aaron in his priestly duties. The rest of the tribe of Levi would assist the congregation in their offerings to the Lord, and assemble and reassemble the tabernacle from camp to camp. The person who offered a sacrifice was not to enter the Tabernacle any further than the *Altar of Sacrifice*. Hence, we learn that the Tabernacle would be divided into 4 parts: (1) The court of the

Gentiles (2) The outer court where male Jews would bring their offering to the Altar of Sacrifice (3) The inner court or the Holy Place where the Levites and Aaron's sons would serve and (4) The Holy of Holies where the Ark of the Covenant stood containing the Golden Pot of Manna, Aaron's Rod that budded, and the two tablets of the testimony (10 commandments).

This incident clearly revealed the Wrath of God against a *stiff-necked* and rebellious people. God killed almost 15,000 Israelites and would have killed them all if Moses and Aaron had not intervened. All of this came from Korah and 250 people who complained about the office of Moses. *Why was God's punishment so severe?*

The penalty of the Korah rebellion was so severe because the rebellion of Korah demonstrated the grim consequences of usurping the authority of God and of those whom He has chosen to be leaders of His people. The problem was not only that Korah rebelled against Moses and Aaron, but in doing so he rebelled against the authority and sovereignty of God. As we study the circumstances in which God's Wrath fell upon Korah in the Old Testament, it must be recognized that God was warning all Christians today that there will be consequences of rebellion and false-Christians in the Church today. Those who would later follow Jesus Christ were warned by Paul to reject such practices. This will be particularly important in the latter days of the Church Age.

[1] This know also, that in the last days perilous times shall come.
[2] For men shall be lovers of their own selves, covetous, boasters, proud, blasphemers, disobedient to parents, unthankful, unholy,
[3] **Without natural affection**, *trucebreakers, false accusers, incontinent, fierce, despisers of those that are good,*
[4] Traitors, heady, high-minded, **lovers of pleasures** *more than lovers of God;*
[5] Having a form of godliness, but denying the power thereof: from such turn away.
[6] For of this sort are they which creep into houses, and lead captive silly women laden with sins, led away with divers lusts,
[7] **Ever learning, and never able to come to the knowledge of the trut***h.*
[8] Now as **Jannes and Jambes** *withstood Moses, so do these also resist the truth: men of corrupt minds, reprobate concerning the faith.*   II Timothy 3: 1-8

False teachers and teachings within the church today project a false gospel of pride, selfishness, jealousy, greed, lust for power, and disregard for the will of God. Just like Korah, many who stand in God's house ignore God's eternal plan for salvation, and are insubordinate to God's appointed authorities. Their end will be the same as Korah's.

Miriam and Her Complaints
Not long after Moses had led the people from Mt. Sinai to the promised land, a woman name *Miriam* complained against Moses. Miriam and Aaron were the sister and brother of Moses. The object of their complaint was evidently that Moses had married an Ethiopian woman…... who was probably black…... after he had been married for almost 40 years to a woman named *Zipporah*. She was the daughter of Jethro who Moses had worked for in the Land of Midian (Exodus 2:31). However, looking further it is clear that this was not the primary complaint of Miriam.
And they said, Hath the LORD indeed spoken only by Moses? hath he not spoken also by us?   Numbers 12:2

Moses had been given complete authority over the people, and God had chosen Moses to speak His words to the people. Miriam and the people did not like Moses constantly telling them what they must do, and some felt that they also had heard from God.

[6] And He said: Hear now my words: If there be a prophet among you, I the LORD will make myself known unto him in a vision, and will speak unto him in a dream.
[7] My servant Moses is not so, who is faithful in all mine house.
[8] With him will I speak mouth to mouth   Numbers 12: 6-8

This question was not one of inquiry because both knew better. It was meant to question the supremacy of Moses, and it was in fact an attack against the authority of Moses, and therefore also against God who appointed Moses to his position of leadership and authority. The Lord turned and departed from Aaron, Miriam and Moses, and as He departed His Wrath fell upon Miriam and she became a leper.

And the cloud departed from off the tabernacle; and, behold, Miriam became leprous, white as snow: and Aaron looked upon Miriam, and, behold, she was leprous.   Numbers 12:10

Why did the Wrath of God fall upon Miriam and not Aaron? Perhaps Miriam was more vocal and assertive than Aaron. Perhaps God did not want to debase the position and authority of Aaron who was the High priest. In any case, Miriam was struck down with leprosy, which was the most devastating societal disease at the time.

Both Aaron and Moses immediately pleaded for God to reverse His curse on Miriam.   Leviticus 12:12

Let her not be as one dead, of whom the flesh is half consumed   Numbers 12:12

Both Aaron and Moses immediately pleaded for God to reverse His curse on Miriam.

And Moses cried unto the LORD, saying: Heal her now, O God, I beseech thee.
Numbers 12:13

In a rare case of mercy and grace, God relented. He told Miriam to remove herself from the camp for a period of 7 days (Numbers 12:15). This she did and the entire group waited for her redemption (Numbers 12:16). At the end of 7 days, Miriam was restored to her former self and the exodus was resumed.

Joshua and the Seven Spies
The next incident that we will discuss is well known to most bible students. Moses was leading the Nation of Israel from Mt. Sinai to the Land of Canaan. God stopped his march in the Wilderness of Paran, and there they pitched camp (Numbers 12:16). God told Moses to select 12 men....one from each of the 12 tribes....and send them to *spy* on the Land of Canaan. The word "spy" is a poor translation of the Greek word *tuwr* which means to *investigate* or *explore*.

[18] And see the land, what it is; and the people that dwelleth therein, whether they be strong or weak, few or many;
[19] And what the land is that they dwell in, whether it be good or bad; and what cities they be that they dwell in, whether in tents, or in strong holds;
[20] And what the land is, whether it be fat or lean, whether there be wood therein, or not. And be ye of good courage, and bring of the fruit of the land. Now the time was the time of the first ripe grapes   Numbers 13: 18-20

This entire exercise was to test the people and determine whether or not they were going to trust God. God wanted to find out if this group of rebellious, complaining and self-serving people were worthy to enter the land. The "spies" were sent out for 40 days and then returned. Not surprising, *all but two* returned a report which questioned God's power and ability to do what He had said he would do. God had promised Abraham and Moses that He would destroy any and all enemies before them, and that the Land of Promise would be theirs. When ten of the twelve spies showed little faith in God by the negative reports that they gave Moses about the land, they were reacting in unbelief to what God had promised them. They did not believe that God could help them, and after hearing the spy's report, people as a whole were persuaded that it was not possible to take the land. As a result, the entire nation was made to wander in the desert for 38 more years, until almost the entire generation of men had died (Numbers 14:30).

Only *Joshua* and *Caleb* brought back a good report and believed that God would lead them to victory. They were the only men from their generation permitted to go into the Promised Land after 38 more years of wandering in the Wilderness. (Numbers 14: 31-32). This is a stark realization of how lack of faith and disbelief can bring death and destruction to any believer. What a shame…The Nation of Israel could have believed God and conquered the land which God had promised to Abraham after only 2 years.

Except for Joshua and Caleb, not one Israelite over the age of reason would ever see the land. This one act of disbelief is a stark reminder of all the years that were wasted as they wandered and died in the wilderness. The astute reader may have noticed that only Joshua and Caleb would live to see the promised land because they both gave a good report. *What about Moses?*

The Wrath of God: Moses and Aaron
Moses is one of the most important Jewish prophets in the Old Testament. He is venerated along with Abraham, Joseph and King David as patriarchs of the Jewish religion. Moses is credited with being obedient to the Lord and liberating the Nation of Israel from Egyptian slavery. He obeyed the Lord and by faith he caused the Red Sea to part, and then used the power of God to drown the chariots of a pursuing Egyptian Pharaoh. It was Moses who ascended Mt. Sinai 8 times and was twice given two tablets of stone upon which God had written the 10 Commandments. It was Moses who supervised building the Tabernacle and then led the Nation of Israel on a 40-year exodus through the Wilderness of Sinai. Considering the faith and obedience by which Moses served God, it is ironic that he was not able to set foot upon the Land of Canaan.

In one of the strangest events recorded in the *Torah*, it is written that Moses had led the Nation of Israel for more than 39 years since they left Egypt, and towards the end of that long journey the Israelites were camped at Kadesh. At that encampment, Miriam the sister of Moses died (Numbers 20:1). According to Jewish tradition (Taanit 9a.), Miriam had been responsible for moving a rock from camp to camp which God had given her to provide water in the wilderness. This is not found in the Holy Scriptures, and whether it is true or not, the story revealed that upon her death the rock supposedly ceased to give water. According to the Torah, this was the 3rd time that Israel complained about the lack of water. The 1st time was at a place called *Marah*. There was water at Marah, but it was bitter. God ordered Moses to cast a tree branch into the water, and it miraculously turned the water sweet. The 2nd time was at a place called *Refidim*. The people were out of water, and Moses called upon God for help. God commanded Moses to *strike the rock* with his staff. Moses did as he was told, and water gushed from the rock. This became known as *Miriam's Rock*, and Jewish legend is that it was carried with the people wherever they went. The 3rd time is when everyone complained about the lack of water in a camp called *Kadesh* and God again heard their cries.

[7] And the LORD spoke unto Moses, saying,
[8] Take the rod, and gather thou the assembly together, thou, and Aaron thy brother, and **speak ye unto the rock** *before their eyes; and it shall give forth his water, and thou shalt bring forth to them water out of the rock: so, thou shalt give the congregation and their beasts drink* Numbers 20: 7-8

Moses and Aaron gathered all of the people before the *Rock of Miribah*, and Moses took the rod into his hand.

And Moses lifted up his hand, and with his rod he **smote the rock twice**: *and the water came out abundantly, and the congregation drank, and their beasts also* Numbers 20:11

The astute reader will immediately note that Moses did not *speak* to the rock, he *smote it twice* with the rod. This is not what God told Moses to do in the Desert of Zin (Numbers 20:1). Because Moses had disobeyed God, both he and Aaron his brother… who was with him… were not allowed to cross the Jordan River (Numbers 20: 20-29). This might seem unfair to Moses. One passionate action by Moses, and God gives him this great punishment? How many times had the Nation of Israel failed God in their journey from Mt. Sinai to the promised land, and God always allowed them to keep going. Now his most faithful servant is severely punished over this seemingly insignificant event? However, if we take a closer look at this incident, we realize why God reacted so violently against Moses and Aaron. God told *both* Moses and his brother Aaron to *speak* to the rock and He would cause a miracle to happen and water would gush from the rock (Numbers 20:8). Instead of both Moses and Aaron speaking to the rock, Moses picked up his rod and struck the rock. By this seemingly innocent incident, both were not allowed to set foot in the land of promise. Moses, Aaron and his brother Eliezer all ascended Mt. Hor and Moses took the garments from Aaron and put them on Eliezer. Aaron died there on Mt. Hor. Moses and Eliezer then descended from the mountain. The people mourned his death for 30 days. At the end of 30 days, Eliezer became the new High Priest. Moses had lost His brother after about 39 years of serving as high priest.

Moses continued to lead God's people towards the Land of Promise. After a few minor skirmishes, Moses and the people arrived at the Plain of Moab. Recall that because of their actions, God told both Moses and Aaron that they would not be allowed to set foot upon the Land of Canaan. It was time for Moses to pay the price for disobedience and be gathered to his fathers. God took Moses up on Mt. Nebo, and after gazing at the Land of Canaan God took Moses to a valley near Mt. Nebo and buried Moses there.

[1] *And Moses went up from the plains of Moab unto the mountain of Nebo, to the top of Pisgah, that is over against Jericho. And the LORD shewed him all the land of Gilead, unto Dan,*

[4] *And the LORD said unto him, This is the land which I swore unto Abraham, unto Isaac, and unto Jacob, saying: I will give it unto thy seed: I have caused thee to see it with thine eyes, but thou shalt not go over thither.*
[5] *So Moses the servant of the LORD died there in the land of Moab, according to the word of the LORD.*
[6] ***And he buried him in a valley*** *in the land of Moab, over against Beth-peor: but no man knoweth of his sepulcher unto this day*   Deuteronomy 34:1, 4-6

So, Moses and his brother Aaron were sentenced to death and not allowed to enter into the promised land because of one, seemingly innocent, act. One might continue to ask *Why? Of what sin were they guilty?* And *why such a harsh punishment?* These questions have been addressed and answered, but the following explanation is as good as I have seen.

> God told Moses and Aaron to *speak* to a rock and water would come out (Numbers 20:8): What? This is a different command by God. Until then, every miracle Moses had done was through actions. He raised his cane in front of the Pharoah: he threw it down and it turned into a serpent. At the Red Sea he raised his arms and the Sea parted. Never had Moses done a miracle at the direction of God through speech. The power of God's spoken word cannot be minimized: God had created the world through speech, and not action (Genesis 1:3: *And God said: Let there be light, and there was light*). Moses, for whatever reason uses his cane as he had done before and he struck the rock (Exodus 17:4). God is furious with Moses with whom he had been speaking "face to face." *Because you did not* believe *in Me, to sanctify Me in the eyes of the children of Israel, therefore you shall not bring this assembly into the Land which I have given them* (Numbers 20:12).

What do we learn? God means it when He gives you a commandment.... if He tells you to do something, that means you already have the capacity to do it. If your own self-doubts lead you to question your ability to follow-through on God's commandments, you not only do not believe in yourself, but you also don't believe in God. *Biblical Hermeneutics*

Jannes and Jambes

Who were *Jannes* and *Jambes*? Not much is known about either individual. Their names appear only once in the entire Holy Bible (II Timothy 3:8) and in the Jewish Talmud. Rabbinical teachings suggest that they may have been two of the soothsayers who challenged Moses and his rod with their own rods which turned into snakes when Moses encountered the Egyptian Pharoah of the Exodus (Exodus 7). Another conjecture is that both Jannes and Jambes were two who joined Aaron and led the people into apostasy at Mt. Sinai when they made the *Golden Calf*. Any positive identification of these two agents of apostasy would only be a guess. We only know that they must have been ungodly and influential people were opponents of the true God. The fate of either wicked individual is not known, they are included just for completeness.

The Conquest of Jericho

We have discussed the promise of God to Abraham concerning the promised land of Canaan. After 40 years of wandering in the wilderness under the leadership of Moses, the Nation of Israel crossed the River Jordan under the new leadership of Joshua. After consecrating themselves by circumcising every male Israelite, Joshua was ready to begin conquering the land. Led by an Angel of the Lord (Joshua 5: 13-15) and the Levites carrying the Tabernacle (Joshua 6: 6-7), Joshua laid siege upon the mighty City of Jericho (Joshua 6:2). The Battle of Jericho, was the first battle fought by the Israelites in the conquest of Canaan. We are told in the Book of Joshua that he sent out two spies in advance to assess the strength and fortifications of Jericho, which was a formidable and well protected city. The spies will have a difficult time and will be detected, but they were to go to the house of Rahab the Harlot where they would be protected (Joshua 2: 1-22). The two spies were hidden from the enemy soldiers in the house of Rahab, and then they returned to Joshua with a good report: *Yes, we can take the city* (Joshua 2: 23-24). The Lord commanded Joshua to surround the city and carry the *Ark of the Covenant* around the walls of Jericho 6 times in 6 days. On the 7th day, they were to march around the city; blow 7 trumpets simultaneously; and then shout (Joshua 6: 3-6). Joshua and all the soldiers did as they were commanded by God, and when the people shouted after circling the city the 7th time, the city walls all fell to the ground. This was nothing less than the mighty, supernatural power of God. Joshua and an army of 4000 attacked the city, burned it to the ground, ravaged the city and returned with all of the spoils of war. All of the gold, silver and precious metal was to be taken to the Tabernacle and dedicated to God. This last command will prove fatal to Achan, his tribe and his entire family.

Achan and the Wrath of God

After conquering Jericho, the Israelites caused much fear and trembling in the Land of Canaan. Jericho was a strong, fortified city, and it had fallen to Joshua and his army in just over 7 days. Even the Israelites were excited.... *If God is for them, who can stand against them?* In the wake of success, Joshua next sets his face toward the town of Ai. Ai was located just east of Bethel. Joshua sends some men to determine the strength of Ai, and they return with a good report. Ai can be easily taken and it should only require about 2000-3000 men (Joshua 7: 2-3). Joshua picks about 3000 men and sends them to Ai, but they soon return with bad news. The men of Ai chased them out of their territory and killed about 36 men. Upon hearing the news, Joshua fell upon his face before the Lord and cried out:

[9] the Canaanites and all the inhabitants of the land shall hear of it, and shall environ us round, and cut off our name from the earth: and what wilt thou do unto thy great name?
[10] And the LORD said unto Joshua, Get thee up; why do you lie upon thy face?
[11] Israel hath sinned, and they have also transgressed my covenant which I commanded them: for they have even taken of the accursed thing, and have also stolen, and dissembled also, and they have put it even among their own
Joshua 7: 9-11

Joshua was not concerned for his dead soldiers but for his own reputation as commander-in-chief (Joshua 7:7). He is worried that the entire Land of Canaan would no longer fear his army and laugh in his face. But the response of God explained that failure was not God's fault but it was due to the disobedience of Achan. He informs Joshua that someone (Achan) had taken gold and silver from the enemy and hid it for himself. *What was so terrible about that?* Recall God had commanded that all spoils of war belong to the Lord, and that they are to be taken to His storehouse (Joshua 6:19). Since God knows everything that is going on, this act of direct disobedience was foolish indeed.

God immediately passes judgment upon Achan. God not only reveals to Joshua exactly why he was defeated, but He also tells Joshua how to handle this transgression.

[12] Therefore the children of Israel could not stand before their enemies, but turned their backs before their enemies, because they were accursed: neither will I be with you any more, except ye destroy the accursed from among you.
[13] Up, sanctify the people, and say, Sanctify yourselves against tomorrow: for thus saith the LORD God of Israel, There is an accursed thing in the midst of thee, O Israel: thou canst not stand before thine enemies, until ye take away the accursed thing from among you.
[14] In the morning therefore ye shall be brought according to your tribes: and it shall be, that the tribe which the LORD taketh shall come according to the families thereof; and the family which the LORD shall take shall come by households; and the household which the LORD shall take shall come man by man.
[15] And it shall be, that he that is taken with the accursed thing shall be burnt with fire, he and all that he hath: because he hath transgressed the covenant of the LORD, and because he hath wrought folly in Israel.
[16] So Joshua rose up early in the morning, and brought Israel by their tribes
Joshua 7: 12-16

All 12 tribes were assembled, and one was the tribe of Judah to which Achan was a member. Joshua confronts Achan and tells him to confess…which he does.

[20] And Achan answered Joshua, and said, Indeed I have sinned against the LORD God of Israel, and thus and thus have I done:
[21] When I saw among the spoils a goodly Babylonish garment, and two hundred shekels of silver, and a wedge of gold of fifty shekels weight, then I coveted them, and took them; and, behold, they are hid in the earth in the midst of my tent, and the silver under it.   Joshua 7: 20-21

Joshua immediately searched the tent of Achan and found the spoils of war hidden beneath the floor. To appease God and avoid his Wrath, Joshua took Achan, his sons, his daughters his cattle and sheep down into the Valley of Achor. There Joshua and everyone else was stoned to death, their bodies burned and their livestock killed (Joshua 7:25).

The story of Achan is a stark reminder of the penalty of sin, which is *death* (Romans 6:23). We also see two other truths plainly illustrated: *First*, sin is never an isolated event…...sin always has an effect that touches others. Achan's sin led to the deaths of thirty-six of his fellow soldiers and defeat for the whole army. *Second,* we can always be sure that our sins will find us out (Numbers 32:23). Hiding the evidence in our tents will not conceal it from God.

The Wrath of God: *Destroys the Enemies of Joshua*
In a series of decisive battles, Joshua systematically destroys his enemies.

- Joshua took Makkedah and completely destroyed everyone
  Joshua 10:28
- Joshua fought against Libnah, and none survived
  Joshua 10: 29-30
- Lachish fell to Joshua and every soul was killed
  Joshua 10: 32
- At Eglon   Joshua 10: 34-35
- At Hebron   Joshua 10: 36-37
- At Debir   Joshua 10: 38-39
- And at Gibeon, Azekah, Makkedah….and all who lived in the valleys, hills and meadows

It is left to the interested bible student to further trace the conquest of Canaan.

So, Joshua took the whole land, according to all that the LORD said unto Moses; and Joshua gave it for an inheritance unto Israel according to their divisions by their tribes. And the land rested from war.   Joshua 11:23

After Joshua had conquered most of the Land of Canaan, he was old and stricken in years; and the LORD said unto him: *Thou art old and stricken in years, and there remains yet very much land to be possessed* (Joshua 13:1).
Nevertheless, Joshua divided the lands he had conquered into 11 separate pieces, one for each of 11 tribes of Israel except for the Levites (Joshua 13:33). In Genesis 12:7 God told Abraham: *To your descendants, I will give this land*. This promise is partially fulfilled in Joshua 13–19. These chapters give a detailed account of the division of the Promised Land among the tribes of Israel. The tribe of Levi received no land as previously dictated by the Lord, and the two sons of Joseph (Ephraim and Manasseh) replaced Joseph and Levi. The land which God promised

to Israel will not all be settled by the Israelites until that covenant is fulfilled in the 1000-year Millennial Kingdom.

Joshua had done almost everything that God commanded him, and at age 110 he died. After his death, the promised land which Joshua had allocated remained in individual segments until King David united the tribes into one cognate kingdom. The Nation of Israel flourished under King David until his death in 970 BC. At that time, his son King Solomon continued to reign over a United Kingdom until Solomon died in the fall of 931 BC.

The Reign of King David
There are several other examples of God's Wrath that resulted in the Kingdom of Israel rebelling against God and His set of laws. We will pass over the period of the Judges and into the period of the kings which ruled over Israel. The people had become more and more sinful as time moved on. They became tired of God and then Judges ruling over them and finally told Samuel: *We want a king like every other nation.* Samuel inquired of God who reluctantly agreed, and Samuel chose Saul as the first King of Israel. Saul was not God's choice, and after David slew Goliath he was chosen by God as the divinely appointed king. The ascension of David to King was not easy. When Saul found out the will of God, he sought to kill David. After a series of encounters, God finally persuaded Saul to fight against the Philistines, and in a battle with the Philistines at Mt. Gilboa, Saul was wounded and committed suicide. David then became King over the unified Kingdom of Israel, and under his leadership the Nation of Israel rose to unprecedented power and strength.

When David died, the United Kingdom passed to his son, Solomon. Solomon started as a righteous king, but he soon became sinful and wicked in the sight of the Lord. Elijah had prophesied that Israel under King Solomon would be divided into two independent kingdoms (I Kings 11: 31-35): The *Northern Kingdom* called Israel which was 10 tribes ruled by his son Jeroboam and the *Southern Kingdom* of Judah ruled by his other son Rehoboam. This division, which took place in approximately 975 BC emerged after the death of Solomon and came about as the people revolted against heavy taxes levied by Solomon and Rehoboam.

The Northern and southern kingdoms did not get along well, and in a short time the Northern Kingdom had degenerated into rebellious, sinful tribes. Their greatest sin was to build altars of worship to foreign gods and turning to *Baal worship*. In time, things got so bad that God said:

Ephraim is joined to idols: let him alone   Hosea 4:17

Fall of the Northern Kingdom

The Lord again and again gave clear warning through prophets such as Jeremiah, Zachariah, Isaiah, Micah, Joel, Amos, Hosea, and others to cease idol worship and immoral practices or they would invoke the Wrath of God. These and other men of God worked tirelessly to bring Israel to her senses and prophesied again and again to a rebellious Israel. Twenty kings ruled the Northern Kingdom, but they were all wicked, having all fallen into Idolatry and Baal Worship. Finally, God moved Assyria to war against the Northern Kingdom and from 726 - 722 BC, the city of Samaria was besieged by the Assyrians. The Northern Kingdom was conquered by the Assyrians, and most of the people were taken into captivity or deported. The Northern Kingdom became known as the *Ten Lost Tribes* after being forcibly removed and deported from their homes and cities. The destruction of Samaria, the Northern Kingdom's capital, was prophesied by Hosea and Micah (Hosea 13:16; Micah 1:6). The Jewish historian Josephus had this to say about the fall of the Northern Kingdom.

> "But the king of Assyria, whose name was Tiglath-Pileser. When he had made an expedition against the Israelites and had overrun all the land of Gilead, and the region beyond Jordan, and the adjoining country, which is called Galilee, and Kadesh, and Hazor.... he made the inhabitants prisoners, and transplanted them into his own kingdom."
> *Josephus, Antiquities of the Jews, Book IX, Chapter 11*

The *Northern Kingdom* of Israel, which the Bible sometimes refers to as *Ephraim*, never recovered from the destruction brought upon it by the Assyrians. The people of the Northern Kingdom were shattered and dispersed as a people, losing their identity as distinct tribes of Israel. The destruction of the Northern Kingdom of Israel and the 10 tribes which lived there has been the subject of much scholarly investigation. There have been many reasons brought forth which *explain* why the Northern Kingdom fell. It is the opinion of this author that while many factors contributed to their total destruction and demise, one overriding fact is clear to those who understand God as a righteous and Holy God who will only tolerate sin and rebellion for so long.

The reason that Israel fell is simple…. God willed and decreed that Israel had sinned and disobeyed Him for the last time, and that the righteous judgment and Wrath of God that fell upon the entire Northern Kingdom was brought about by a rebellious and evil people. They had no excuses…. They had abandoned the same God that saved them from Egyptian slavery, and failed to believe His promises to Abraham and Moses.

It took Assyria almost 20 years to *completely* conquer the Northern Kingdom of Israel. In the ninth year of Hoshea, the king of Assyria took Samaria, and carried Israel away into Assyria. He placed them in Halah and in Habor by the river of Gozan, and in the cities of the Medes. (2 Kings 17:3–6). An Assyrian cuneiform tablet has been found which records that 27,290 captives were taken from Samaria, which was the capital of the Northern Kingdom of Israel.

Make no mistake about it, the Northern Kingdom was carried away to Assyria because they did not obey the voice of the LORD their God but transgressed His covenant. Everything which God had told Moses and the people to do, they rejected, and all that Moses the servant of the LORD had commanded them to do they neither listened nor obeyed. (2 Kings 18:11–12).

The Southern Kingdom had not exactly pleased God either. With the Northern Kingdom in ruins and no threat of any invasion or aggression from the North, the Southern Kingdom made a fatal mistake. Rather than recognize that the Northern Kingdom had been the subject of God's Wrath, Judah became just as bad as the Northern Kingdom.

Fall of the Southern Kingdom

It was not long before the Southern Kingdom of Judah…whose capital was in Jerusalem…. also slid into pagen practices, debauchery and sin. Finally, God had enough of their rebellion also and in 587/586 BC God brought Nebuchadnezzar and the Babylonian Empire against Judah. In 586 BC Jerusalem was overrun by the Babylonians, the City of Jerusalem was ransacked and destroyed; and most of the Israelites carried away into Babylonian captivity for 70 years. Nebuchadnezzar also burned and destroyed Solomon's Temple; Carrying away the furniture, gold and silver. The Ark of the Covenant contained the rod of Aaron which budded, a golden pot of manna and the 10 commandments. It is generally believed that the

Ark disappeared in 586 BC when Jerusalem and Solomon's Temple were both ransacked and burned. Where the Ark is now is anyone's guess, but it has been long believed that it disappeared shortly before the temple was burned by the Babylonians. In Rabbinic literature, the final disposition of the Ark is disputed. A late 2nd-century rabbinic work known as the *Tosefta* states that Josiah hid the Ark in somewhere in caves on the Temple Mount. Rabbi Eliezer and Rabbi Shimon, in the same rabbinic work, state that the Ark was actually taken into Babylon. According to a non-canonical book called II Maccabees the prophet Jeremiah gave orders that the Tent of Meeting and the ark should go with him. He supposedly took the Ark to Mt. Nebo.. When he reached the mountain, Jeremiah found a cave where he hid the ark. Jeremiah supposedly said: *The place shall remain unknown until God finally gathers his people together and shows mercy to them.* The truth is that no one knows where the Ark of the Covenant was taken or if it still exists today.

The Ark carried into the Temple from the early 15th century *Très Riches Heures du Duc de Berry*

One might ask the question of why, when Assyria conquered the Northern Kingdom of Israel, they did not continue south and then also destroy the Southern Kingdom of Judah. This question was answered in a prophecy written by Isaiah.

[33] Therefore thus saith the LORD concerning the king of Assyria, He shall not come into this city, nor shoot an arrow there nor come before it with shields, nor cast a bank against it.
[34] By the way that he came, by the same shall he return, and shall not come into this city, saith the LORD.
[35] For I will defend this city to save it for mine own sake, and for my servant David's sake.
*[36] Then the angel of the LORD went forth, and smote in the camp of the Assyrians a **hundred and fourscore and five thousand**: and when they arose early in the morning, behold, they were all dead corpses.*   Isaiah 37: 33-38

This is a prophecy directed toward Assyria and its desire to attack the Judah and the City of Jerusalem after they had finally conquered Israel. Isaiah plainly prophesies that the Assyrians would not attack Jerusalem or Judah because God will divinely protect His Holy City, His Holy Temple, and a remnant of the people that He has called to Himself. However, there is a hidden message in the words of Isaiah…the Assyrians would not come against the Southern Kingdom, but these words did not say that some other Kingdom would not come against Judah if His people would not hearken to His word.

When the Northern Kingdom fell, the Southern Kingdom was ruled by King Hezekiah who was a man of God. Under his leadership the Southern Kingdom experienced religious revival, but when Hezekiah died he was succeeded by *Manasseh*, who was evil and turned his face away from God. Manasseh was the wickedest king to ever rule over Judah, and he ruled longer than any other king in the Southern Kingdom. The kingdom never recovered from the apostacy of Hezekiah, and when he died his son Amon ruled and continued the downward spiral of Judah. Amon was soon assassinated by Josiah who temporarily turned back to God when he discovered a copy of the Law of Moses in Solomon's Temple (II Chronicles 34:14). The destruction of Judah and Solomon's Temple was prophesied by Zephaniah. Zephaniah probably lived during the time of Jeremiah, and he joined him in warning the kingdom of Judah of impending destruction. Zephaniah also prophesied about the latter days and warned of calamities to come before the Second Coming of the Savior (Zephaniah 1).

By 610 BC, the Assyrian Empire weakened and was succeed by the Babylonian Empire. The decline and eventual collapse of the powerful Assyrian Empire was part of God's plan for the eventual destruction of Jerusalem and Judah by the Babylonian Empire. After the rule of King Josiah, there was no hope for Judah. The last 3 kings who ruled over the Southern Kingdom (Jehoiakim, Zedekiah and Jehoahaz) were all evil and spelled the end of God's patience. Led by Nebuchadnezzar, the Babylonian Empire swept down upon Jerusalem in 597 BC and a temporary truce was obtained. In 586 BC the Babylonians once again invaded Judah, and this time the city pf Jerusalem was ransacked, burned and all but the very old and young were deported to Babylon. Solomon's temple was burned to the ground and all of the furniture in the Tabernacle as seized and taken to Babylon. The fall of the Southern Kingdom and the destruction of Solomon's Temple was a direct result of God's people ignoring His commands and apostatizing. However, one must realize that while the Wrath of God permitted Judah to fall, it was not permanent. God had made an unconditional Covenant with Abraham that his seed (singular) would not perish.

*And I will establish my covenant between me and thee and thy **seed** after thee in their generations for an everlasting covenant, to be a God unto thee, and to thy **seed** after thee*   Genesis 17:7

*And in thy **seed** shall all the nations of the earth be blessed; because thou hast obeyed my voice.*   Genesis 22:18

*Now to Abraham and his **seed** were the promises made. He saith not and to seeds, as of many; but as of one: And to thy seed, which is Christ*   Galatians 3:16

The seed of Abraham which would bless the entire world was Jesus Christ, who would come from the tribe of Judah.

The Babylonian exile would last 70 years. *Why 70 years?* This period of time is a direct consequence of Jewish time being measured by successive periods of 7 years. Seven periods of 7 years (49 years) are called a *Sabbatical Cycle*, and the 50th year following a sabbatical Cycle is called a *Year of Jubilee*. Every *Year of Jubilee* was to be a year of rest for the land. No crops could be planted or harvested in that year. Evidently, Israel never observed a Year of Jubilee for 70 cycles of 50 years. The Southern Kingdom paid for this transgression by being carried away into Babylonian exile for 70 consecutive years (II Chronicles 36:21). The destruction of Jerusalem, Solomon's Temple, and the Babylonian exile, is never called the Wrath of God in the Holy Scriptures but it obviously was and we identify it as such.

Chapter 4

Judgments and Wrath of God in the New Testament

The Dispensation of Grace

The circumstances that prompted God to unleash His wrath upon mankind in the Old Testament are not easily found in the New Testament. It night be conjectured that this is true because of the way that God interacted with his creation in the Old Testament and how he interacts with man in the New Testament. In most of the Old Testament, God was dealing directly with mankind which He had created. He often made a *unilateral* and *unconditional covenant* with mankind, involving covenant promises which could not be declared null and void. This does not mean that God did not release His wrath upon individuals or groups of individuals at various points in time in different Dispensations. In those cases, fulfillment of covenant promises could be delayed to another point in time but could not be cancelled. God himself created Adam and Eve and walked and talked with them in the Garden of Eden (Dispensation of Innocence). After they both sinned and were banned from the Garden, there was no written law and God ruled in a *theocracy*. A theocracy is a form of government in which one or more deities are recognized as supreme ruling authorities. A contemporary example is the Vatican, and the pope is the ruling authority. God interacted with man by appearing to them in various forms or in different ways. When God destroyed all mankind except for Noah, his 3 sons, and their four wives; He continued to reign as a sovereign God and His reign was once again a *theocracy*. After the flood, there was essentially a new beginning. Just as before the flood, when all mankind descended from Adam.... now every man and woman descended from Noah and his 3 sons. Of course, Noah was a descendent of Adam so the original sin was propagated through Noah and his sons. The seed of Noah became exceedingly wicked, and so God chose Abraham to spawn His chosen people, the *Nation of Israel*. All this time, the form of human government was a theocracy.... But that was soon to change. When mankind once again apostatized and became wicked, God caused them to be slaves and indentured servants. God rescued Israel from Egyptian slavery, and He then gave His laws to the nation of Israel at Mt. Sinai. Sometime later, those of the Nation of Israel who chose to live under the Law became known as *Jews*. The first appearance of the word "Jew" in the Bible is in Kings II 16:6. This term was derived from the *Men of Yehuda*. According to the Book of Genesis, Yehuda was the fourth of the six sons of Jacob and Leah, and was the direct progenitor of the Tribe of Judah.

This history of the Jews provides us with a deeper understanding of how God was personally aligned with the Jews. They were His chosen people in the Old Testament, and there were only two classes of people: *Jews* and *Gentiles*. … nothing else. God ruled in a theocracy, but to carry out His eternal plan he chose exceptionally strong men of God to lead mankind and carry out His wishes. Noah, Abraham, Joseph, Moses David and Joshua were all sinners as was every other man, but they recognized their failures and sincerely asked God to forgive them. Not only did they ask for forgiveness in prayer, but they had faith that God would redeem them from their sins by sending a *Messiah*. This is basically what set them apart from all other men.

There is one other overriding reason why God treated mankind differently in the Old Testament than how He now treats man under the New Covenant. Throughout this study one fact has been presented that has explained the behavior of God in different periods of time during which God dealt with man in special and unique ways: These periods of time are called *dispensations*. It is impossible to rightly divide the word of God and understand His eternal plan for mankind without understanding the nature and boundaries of each dispensation. We are currently living in the *Dispensation of Grace* which is also called the *Church Age*, and it is radically different from the 5 dispensations that span the Old Testament. There has only been one thing that unifies the relationship between God and Man throughout history….and that is *faith*.

For what saith the scripture? Abraham believed God, and it was counted unto him for righteousness   Romans 4:3

Under the new covenant, there are still only two classes of people: *Believers* and *Unbelievers*. In the current dispensation of grace, there is no difference in Jews or Gentiles. Anyone who has been born since God created Adam is born in sin (Original sin of Adam). Since Christ would not appear until about 30 AD, every man and woman who existed in the Old Testament had no hope of finding salvation and eternal life since there was no way to attain permanent forgiveness of sins. However, those who died in the faith of Abraham did not die without hope. They believed that God would someday send a Messiah…a redeemer…who would permanently forgive sins for all who believed when God chose to do so. This would launch a radically different Dispensation by which all mankind…past, present and future would have their sins forgiven. These men and women died in the *Faith of Abraham.* They all believed and expected to find forgiveness of sins and attain eternal life: They would be saved by *faith plus nothing*.

All Old Testament and New Testament sons and daughters of God who are guaranteed eternal life believe(d) that a redeemer would be sent by God to forgive all sins. This *must* be true because God cannot tolerate sin in His prescence. In the Old Testament all men and women died in faith that God would send such a redeemer, and that man was known as the *Messiah*. They did not know the name of that man or exactly when he would come…but men of faith had an unwavering faith that a Messiah sent by God would one day appear. Of course, that man was *Jesus Christ* the *Son of God.* Every New Covenant Christian, except for a few who personally walked and talked with Jesus Christ in the 1st century AD, is saved in *exactly* the same way….*by faith*. No one today has seen Christ, but all born-again Christians believe that He was the Son of God who died for our sins.

All of this leads to the conclusion that the nature and severity of Gods Wrath against his people here on the earth were dramatically different before and after the Cross of Calvary. The cross is the great dividing line between all time. Christ was the perfect Lamb of God who once and permanently enabled the forgiveness of sins and *justified* people of faith. The Great Flood came as a vehicle of God's Wrath upon all the people of this earth but eight. Sodom and Gomorrah could have been saved if only 10 righteous people of faith could have been found, and the Northern and Southern Kingdoms of Israel and Judah would not have been almost completely destroyed if men would have trusted in God and followed His commands. In stark contrast, men and women who live and die under the New Covenant are judged as *individuals*. Salvation is one person at a time by individual faith in Jesus Christ, and not by birth or religious affiliation.

*whosoever **believeth** in him should not perish, but have eternal life*   John 3:15

Under both the New Covenant and the Old Covenant, there is no corporate salvation or corporate eternal life. Forgiveness of sin and eternal life is now available to Jews who became Jewish by a *physical birth* by being *born-again* into the body of Jesus Christ by the holy Spirit, and this is an *individual* choice. Man is a free moral agent and God will allow every individual to make a personal choice. This is not to imply that the Wrath of God has been permanently finished. It does imply that there will be a judgment of rewards (Bema Seat judgment) after the Battle of Armageddon, and of death and punishment (Great White Throne Judgment) which will take place after the 1000-year Millennial Kingdom ends.

All Old Testament *Wrath of God* fell upon those who ignored His commands and the Law. When the Law was replaced by faith and grace, violation of any Old

Covenant law or command is *permanently* forgiven by the *blood of Christ*. Accountability and punishment in the Old Testament were much more severe and immediate than after the Dispensation of Grace began. The Wrath of God is not angry retribution against those who have offended or disobeyed Him, but it is His righteous judgment against those who sin and violate His righteous standards. Everyone will be judged, either at the end of this current Church Age or at the end of the Millennial Kingdom.

For we must all appear before the judgment seat of Christ; that every one may receive the things done in his body, according to that he hath done, whether it be good or bad   II Corinthians 5:10

Finally, note that Jesus Christ sacrificed His perfect, sinless life for us of His own volition. He had no sin(s) to forgive. He did it to fulfill the eternal plan of God and to please His Father. As a result of His final and vicarious sacrifice, Jesus Christ has been placed in a preeminent position

[16] *For by him were all things created, that are in heaven, and that are in earth, visible and invisible, whether they be thrones, or dominions, or principalities, or powers: all things were created by him, and for him:*
[17] *And he is before all things, and by him all things consist.*
[18] *And he is the head of the body, the church: who is the beginning, the firstborn from the dead; that in all things he might have the preeminence.*
[19] *For it pleased the Father that in him should all fulness dwell*
Colossians 1: 16-19

Part of the preeminence of Christ is that God has placed Him in charge of all judgment and condemnation of those who refuse to believe.

And He commanded us to preach unto the people, and to testify that it is He which was ordained of God to be the Judge of quick and dead.   Acts 10:42

That is what the Apostle Paul meant when he wrote in Romans 4:15: *Where there is no law (of Moses) there is no transgression.* He further explained:

[20] *Therefore by the deeds of the law there shall no flesh be justified in his sight: for by the law is the knowledge of sin.*
[21] *But now the righteousness of God without the law is manifested, being witnessed by the law and the prophets;*
[22] *Even the righteousness of God which is by faith of Jesus Christ unto all and upon all them that believe: for there is no difference:*
[23] *For all have sinned, and come short of the glory of God;*

[24] *Being justified freely by his grace through the redemption that is in Christ Jesus:*   Romans 3: 20-24

If wrath is synonymous with revenge, it might be hard to reconcile the Wrath of God with Righteous Revenge. But if the wrath of God is simply his righteous judgment against sinful humanity, then there is really no conflict between the two. The Wrath of God against sinful man in the Old Testament is distinctly different than the Wrath of God or the Wrath of Jesus Christ in the New Testament. Both are one in purpose, plan and intent that all men would be saved and worship God, but in examining God's wrath against man in the New Testament it is clear that God does not react to the disobedience and sin of man here upon this earth under the New Covenant as He did under the Old Covenant. In reflecting upon the difference of how both covenants operated and were instituted, there are clues of why and how God deals with disobedience and sin in the Old Covenant verses the New Covenant.

The Old Covenant was based upon the *law* and *works*, while the New Covenant is based upon *faith* and *grace*. In the Old Covenant, the law could *not* be violated without sinning against God and his character. There was no immediate and permanent forgiveness of sin in the Old Testament. Forgiveness of sin would not come until Jesus Christ died upon the Cross of calvary. Anyone covered by the blood of Christ would certainly be held accountable for both good deeds and bad deeds under the New Covenant at the *Bema Seat Judgment* of all believers, but transgression of the law under the New Covenant does not automatically condemn anyone. The only condemnation which was permanent was failure to accept Jesus Christ as Lord and Savior by *faith*. All Old Testament men and women who died in the faith of Abraham believed that one day a Messiah would be sent from God to redeem their sins. All Old Testament men and women who died *without* the faith of Abraham will be condemned and sentenced to the 2nd death which will be eternity in the Lake of Burning Fire, just as all New Covenant unbelievers.

For the wages of sin is death   Romans 6:23

For whosoever shall keep the whole law, and yet offend in one point, he is guilty of all   James 2:10

I am the way, the truth, and the life: no man cometh unto the Father, but by me John 14:6

There was no escape from the law, and when broken there was no immediate forgiveness. There was one one way that one could find eternal life and forgiveness, and that was by a promised Messiah and Redeemer who would one day be sent from God to permanently forgive sins. Of course, we now know that the only person who could ever accomplish that was Jesus Christ the Son of God.

Jesus Christ would not appear until the 1st century AD, and so under the Old Covenant no one died with their sins forgiven. The Jews were able to live year by year by temporary *atonement* of sins enabled by sacrificial offerings of bulls and goats. Day after day and year after year, sacrifices of bulls and goats were only a covering for sins until Jesus Christ permanently settled the sin issue on the Cross of Calvary. In the Old Testament, God dealt with sin by releasing His righteous judgment and wrath upon man, when sin abounded so much that His righteous judgment was necessary. Contrast the way that God reacted to sin in the Old Testament with how He deals with sin under the New Covenant. God was so pleased with the obedience and ultimate sacrifice of Jesus Christ, that He passed all judgment and Wrath onto His son to honor Him.

[26] For as the Father hath life in himself; so hath he given to the Son to have life in himself;
[27] **And hath given him authority to execute judgment** *also, because he is the Son of man.*
[28] Marvel not at this: for **the hour is coming***, in the which all that are in the graves shall hear his voice,*
[29] And shall come forth; they that have done good, unto the resurrection of life; and they that have done evil, unto the resurrection of damnation   John 5:26-29

Carefully studying the 3.5 years of the Redeeming work of Jesus Christ, we cannot find even one instance where the Wrath of God or the Wrath of the Son fell upon sinful man before the Great tribulation and the end of the church age. God withholds His wrath to honor his Son, and the Son withholds His wrath until the Age of Grace is finished. The Book of Revelation is full of God's Wrath (Revelation 11:18, Revelation 14:10, 19, Revelation 16:1, 19, Revelation 18:3 and Revelation 19:15), and in one instance the Wrath of the Lamb (Revelation 6:16).

It appears that during His earthly ministry of 3.5 years, Jesus Christ lost his temper on only two occasions, both on the same day. The day after Jesus entered

Jerusalem on *Palm Sunday*, Jesus arose from the house of Lazarus and was going to the temple to teach and heal the masses that had gathered there. As He passed a *Fig Tree* he was hungry, but when He examined the fig tree it had no fruit. Jesus was distraught and he declared: *No man eat fruit of thee hereafter forever* (Mark 11:14). In examining the context of this act, it is clear that Christ was using the barren fig tree as a type of Israel, and the lack of fruit represented Israel as a nation in unbelief and bearing no fruit. Wrath and judgment would fall upon Israel as a nation later. This is why Jesus said in Matthew 3:

And now also the axe is laid unto the root of the trees: Therefore, every tree which bringeth not forth good fruit is hewn down, and cast into the fire   Matthew 3:10

That same day when Christ entered the temple to teach and heal, upon entering the temple He found the *moneychangers* buying and selling animals for sacrifice. In a rare display of anger, he hated what was taking place, overturned the moneychangers' tables, and ran them out of the temple because it dishonored His Father's house.

My house shall be called of all nations the house of prayer, but ye have made it a den of thieves   Matthew 11:17

These were the only recorded incidents in the entire 3.5-year ministry of Jesus Christ that He exercised righteous anger.

In light of what is found in the New Testament concerning the outpouring of Wrath, we will describe *three* different events in the Book of Revelation in which the righteous indignation of God and His Son will come to pass:

(1) The wilderness Judgment of God upon His chosen people, called the *Rod Judgment*
(2) The *Sheep and Goats Judgment* (Judgment of the Nations)
(3) The *Great White Throne Judgment* of all unbelievers.

It should be noted here that *none* of these Judgments actually represent the *Wrath of God* or of the *Son*. Both the *Bema Seat Judgment and the Great White Throne Judgment* are concerned with only one question: *What did each individual do with Jesus Christ who was the Son of God and died for all sins.* The *Rod Judgment* will take place immediately after the Battle of Armageddon. The *Judgment of the*

Nations will take place following the end of the Great Tribulation and the current Church age, and will only be concerned with how people of the nations treated the Jews during the 3.5 years of Satan's persecution of all mankind. Except for the *Rod Judgment* of the Jews by God, it appears that all other judgments will be by our Lord Jesus Christ.

For the Father judges no man, but hath committed all judgment unto the Son
John 5:22

And he commanded us to preach unto the people, and to testify that it is He which was ordained of God to be the Judge of quick and dead   Acts 10:42

I charge thee therefore before God, and the Lord Jesus Christ, who shall judge the quick and the dead at his appearing and his kingdom   II Timothy 4:1

> *Authors Note*: There is one other judgment which is known to almost every Christian. It is the *Bema Seat Judgment* for the rewards of all true believers from both the New Covenant and the Old Testament. This is not a judgment of wrath and condemnation and therefore will not be discussed. The interested scholar may wish to read: Phillips; The Book of Revelation: *Mysteries Revealed*

The Wilderness Rod Judgment

In Revelation 12, John sees a great battle which is taking place, in heaven, between Satan and his fallen angels and Michael and his holy angels. After this great heavenly battle takes place and Satan is defeated, Michael and his army of angels will be banished from heaven and confined to this earth (Revelation 12:9). Satan will be furious, and immediately start to persecute all Jews and Christians (Revelation 12:12, 17). Recognizing that their life is in danger, the Jews will flee from Jerusalem to a place prepared for them by God in the wilderness (Revelation 12:14). Satan will pursue these Jews, but as they flee from Satan, God will supernaturally rescue them by causing a flood to swallow up the *Wrath of Satan* in a great earthly chasm (The location of where God will protect the fleeing remnant is not revealed in Revelation 12, but God will supernaturally protect them there for 3.5 years from the Wrath of Satan, which are the 7 Trumpet Judgments). Exactly who will flee to the wilderness or how they will be chosen is not revealed in Revelation 12, but they will remain there until after the 7 trumpet Judgments (The Wrath of Satan), the 7 Bowl Judgments (The Wrath of God) and the Battle of Armageddon (The Second Advent of Jesus Christ) has been completed. After the

Battle of Armageddon has been fought and won by Jesus Christ, God will suddenly appear to His beloved Jews in the wilderness and execute what is called the *Rod Judgment* upon all of the people of Israel that have been under His protection for 3.5 years. This rather obscure and seldom recognized event was prophesied by Ezekiel long ago.

> **[33]** *As I live, saith the Lord GOD, surely with a mighty hand, and with a stretched out arm, and with fury poured out, will I rule over you:*
> **[34]** *And I will bring you out from the people, and will gather you out of the countries wherein ye are scattered, with a mighty hand, and with a stretched out arm, and with fury poured out.*
> **[35]** *And I will bring you into the wilderness of the people, and there will I plead with you face to face.*
> **[36]** *Like as I pleaded with your fathers in the wilderness of the land of Egypt, so will I plead with you, saith the Lord GOD.*
> **[37]** *And I will cause you to pass under the rod, and I will bring you into the bond of the covenant:*
> **[38]** *And I will purge out from among you the rebels, and them that transgress against me: I will bring them forth out of the country where they sojourn, and they shall not enter into the land of Israel: and ye shall know that I am the LORD.*   Ezekiel 20: 33-38

Most scholars identify this prophecy with the Babylonian exile and the return of the Jews to Israel after 70 years, but this cannot be true for the following reasons.
1. God himself will rule over this remnant (Ezekiel 20: 33)
2. The people that God will rescue will be out of countries (plural) and not just Babylon (Ezekiel 20:34)
3. God will ratify a covenant with those who will pass under His Rod of Judgment (Ezekiel 20:37)
4. This remnant is not saved and protected to inherit the promised land or return to Israel but will serve Him (Ezekiel 20:38)

Here we see that God will cause all of the children of Israel who have survived the last half of Daniel's 70th week to come into the wilderness to *pass under the rod. What is this rod?* In ancient times the sheepherder would line up all of his flock and cause them to pass one at a time through a narrow gate under a rod. As they came under the rod, he would count them and separate the ones who were blemished and unfit from those who had not failed the test. Those who pass under

God's *Rod of Judgment* will serve Him during the Millennial Kingdom. While God is bringing His *bride* to return to a covenant relationship with Him, Christ is preparing to judge the nations. Before Christ can judge the nations, He travels south toward *Edom* and *Petra* to reclaim the remnant that had fled there after the antichrist and his armies attacked Jerusalem in what Van Kampen called the *Jerusalem Campaign* just before the Battle of Armageddon. Those who Christ will judge have likely retreated to Bozrah and the ancient fortress city of *Petra*. This act is recorded in a strange and obscure passage found in Isaiah 63 and is likely related to Revelation 12: 13-16.

[1] *Who is this that cometh from Edom, with dyed garments from Bozrah? this that is glorious in his apparel, travelling in the greatness of his strength? I that speak in righteousness, mighty to save.*
[2] *Wherefore art thou red in thine apparel, and thy garments like him that treads in the winefat?*
[3] *I have trodden the winepress alone; and of the people there was none with me: for I will tread them in mine anger, and trample them in my fury; and their blood shall be sprinkled upon my garments, and I will stain all my raiment.*
[4] *For the day of vengeance is in mine heart, and the year of my redeemed is come.* Isaiah 63: 1-4

From this prophecy, we see that Christ is:

- Coming from Edom and Bozrah.
- He is displaying great strength.
- He speaks righteously.
- His apparel is stained red with (sprinkled) blood.

The best interpretation of this passage is that Christ has *already trodden the winepress*, and it is this Battle at Armageddon which has stained His garments with blood. In Revelation 14 we are told:

[18] *And another angel came out from the altar, which had power over fire; and cried with a loud cry to him that had the sharp sickle, saying, Thrust in thy sharp sickle, and gather the clusters of the vine of the earth; for her grapes are fully ripe.*
[19] *And the angel thrust in his sickle into the earth, and gathered the vine of the earth, and cast it into* **the great winepress** *of the wrath of God.*
[20] *And the winepress was trodden without the city, and blood came out of the*

winepress, even unto the horse bridles, by the space of a thousand and six hundred furlongs.   Revelation 14: 18-20

Who *treads the winepress*? In language very similar to that used in Isaiah (Isaiah 63:3), we are told it will be Jesus Christ.

[13] And he was clothed with a vesture dipped in blood: and his name is called The Word of God.
[14] And the armies which were in heaven followed him upon white horses, clothed in fine linen, white and clean.
[15] And out of his mouth goeth a sharp sword, that with it he should smite the nations: and he shall rule them with a rod of iron: and **he treads the winepress** *of the fierceness and wrath of Almighty God.*   Revelation 19: 13-15

The Greek phrase translated **dipped in blood** could also be translated *splattered in blood*. Comparing scripture to scripture, it is not conclusive but it is quite likely that this person who is *coming from Edom and Bozrah* (Isaiah 63:1) is our Lord Jesus Christ. His garments are splattered with the blood of the Antichrist and his armies which were totally annihilated. It appears that this trip to Bozrah takes place immediately *following* the battle of Armageddon on Tishri 10, and *before* the Feast of Tabernacles on Tishri 15-22. It may directly precede the Rod Judgment of God just discussed. *After* he returns in blood-stained garments and judges the Jews in the Rod judgment, the *nations of the world* will be gathered to Jerusalem before the throne of Christ, and all will take place in the judgment of the *Sheep and the Goats*.

Judgment of the Nations: *The Sheep and Goats*

[31] When the Son of man shall come in his glory, and all the holy angels with him, then shall he sit upon the throne of his glory:
[32] And before him shall be gathered all nations: and he shall separate them one from another, as a shepherd divides his sheep from the goats:
[33] And he shall set the sheep on his right hand, but the Father, inherit the kingdom prepared for you from the foundation of the world: goats on the left.
Matthew 25: 31-33

The judgment of the *sheep and goats* will separate people from all of the other nations who have survived the Great tribulation into two groups: One group will go into the millennial kingdom, and the other group will be cast into the lake of burning fire. The criteria are given by Christ Himself in Matthew 25: 35-46. It is how the people of the nations treated *my brethren* during the *Time of Great tribulation and persecution.*

[34] Then shall the King say unto them on his right hand, Come, ye blessed of my Father, inherit the kingdom prepared for you from the foundation of the world:
[35] For I was an hungry, and ye gave me meat: I was thirsty, and ye gave me drink: I was a stranger, and ye took me in:
[36] Naked, and ye clothed me: I was sick, and ye visited me: I was in prison, and ye came unto me.
[37] Then shall the righteous answer him, saying, Lord, when saw we thee an hungry, and fed thee? or thirsty, and gave thee drink?
[38] When saw we thee a stranger, and took thee in? or naked, and clothed thee?
[39] Or when saw we thee sick, or in prison, and came unto thee?
[40] And the King shall answer and say unto them, Verily I say unto you, Inasmuch as ye have done it unto one of the least of these my brethren, ye have done it unto me.   Matthew 25: 35-40

This is an astonishing statement by Matthew concerning his Lord and Savior Jesus Christ. Matthew calls Him *the king*. He has returned and He will sit upon His throne of glory and rule over all creation. God has ordained this to be so because only Jesus Christ could redeem man and be the perfect sacrificial Lamb of God. He alone is worthy to sit upon the Throne of David and rule and reign. This is after the Church age has ended, and the *Righteous Judge* will determine who will enter into the Millennial Kingdom based upon how they have treated *His brethren*.

Many will reply: *What are you talking about? I never gave you food, shelter or clothes and I am just now beholding your glory.* Should anyone be astonished to hear such an account of their own actions? Our Lord and savior who we all long to see will simply respond: *Ye did all this unto Me.* Those who will be gathered to His right, *just as a mother hen would put her chicks under her wing*, might honestly respond......No, it cannot be: We never saw you and we never gave you anything but our faith...*Are you sure*? Those who the Lord will reward can only imagine being overcome by grace. Those who will be rewarded have lived not only in faith but by love for others who are less fortunate than they were. In can be well imagined that these saints lived as Abraham did.... They did not hide their wealth under a rock or store up what they were given while here on Earth, but they were blessed to be a blessing.

[19] Lay not up for yourselves treasures upon earth, where moth and rust doth corrupt, and where thieves break through and steal:
[20] But lay up for yourselves treasures in heaven, where neither moth nor rust doth corrupt, and where thieves do not break through nor steal
Matthew 6: 19-20

The Millennial Dispensation
The Millennial Dispensation is the 7th and last of the 7 Dispensations of time that frame the eternal plan of God. It will last 1000 years and will be a time that God will rule and reign over all the world from his Throne room which will be situated on a newly formed plateau just outside the current site of Jerusalem. He will sit upon the Throne of David and will be assisted by a resurrected King David. It will be a glorious period of time during which the Land of Canaan which God had long ago promised to Abraham will be inhabited by 10 tribes of Israel (The interested bible student is referred to Phillips: *Life After the Great Tribulation*).

When the Millennial Disposition finally comes to an end several monumental events will take place in rapid succession.: (1) Satan will be released from the Bottomless pit where he has been held captive for 1000-years (2) Satan will immediately assemble all of his demons and unbelievers from every point in the globe and (3) Satan and his army will march upon Jerusalem to destroy the city and its inhabitants in what we will call *Satan's Last Stand* (4) Suddenly, Jesus Christ and His father will intercept the evil forces of Satan in the plains outside of Jerusalem and (5) god will quickly and destroy all of His enemies. Satan will be cast into the Lake of burning fire where the Antichrist and the False Prophet have been for the last 1000-years. Unbelievers from all ages past will be assembled before the Throne of God to be Judged for their actions and beliefs. They will be joined by those true believers who have died during the Millennial Kingdom. All whose names who are not written in the Book of Life will be cast into the Lake of Burning Fire where they will suffer for all eternity.

The Great White Throne Judgment
Those unbelievers who will be judged at the *Great White Throne* will be not be judged for rewards but for the degree of punishment which they will experience for all eternity in the *Lake of Burning Fire*. This is called the **second death** for all *unbelievers* from the first Adam to the end of the 1000-year reign of Jesus Christ in the millennial kingdom (Revelation 20:14). They have made their choice, and their

life here on earth is to be judged and found wanting at the *Great White Throne Judgment*, which will take place immediately following the 1000-year Millennial Kingdom. When the Battle of Armageddon ends, Satan will be cast into the bottomless pit for 1000 years (Revelation 20:1-3), and when the thousand years are over Satan will be loosed out of his prison for ***a little while*** (Rev 20:3) to gather his forces from all over the world. Immediately preceding the Great White Throne Judgment, Satan will make one last, futile attempt to destroy Jerusalem and all of the Jews he can find.

[7] *And when the thousand years are expired, Satan shall be loosed out of his prison,*
[8] *And shall go out to deceive the nations which are in the four quarters of the earth, Gog and Magog, to gather them together to battle: the number of whom is as the sand of the sea.*
[9] *And they went up on the breadth of the earth, and compassed the camp of the saints about, and the beloved city: and fire came down from God out of heaven, and devoured them.*
[10] *And the devil that deceived them was cast into the lake of fire and brimstone, where the beast and the false prophet are, and shall be tormented day and night for ever and ever.*   Revelation 20: 7-10

Satan will call all unbelievers to him when he is released from the *Bottomless Pit*, and he will march upon *Jerusalem*. This will be called *Satan's Last Stand*. Before Satan can get there, God himself will intercept his forces and destroy them all. The battle must be brief, because it is barely given mention in Revelation 20:9. However, the *Great White Throne Judgment* is described in some detail.
[11] *And I saw a great white throne, and him that sat on it, from whose face the earth and the heaven fled away; and there was found no place for them.*
[12] *And I saw the dead, small and great, stand before God; and the books were opened: and another book was opened, which is the book of life: and the dead were judged out of those things which were written in the books, according to their works.*
[13] *And the sea gave up the dead which were in it; and death and hell delivered up the dead which were in them: and they were judged every man according to their works.*
[14] *And death and hell were cast into the lake of fire.* **This is the second death**.
[15] *And whosoever was not found written in the book of life was cast into the lake of fire.*   Revelation 20: 11-15

Following the Great White Throne Judgment, Death and Hell were *cast into the Lake of Fire*, and the last enemy to be destroyed will be *death and hell* (Gehenna). The apostle Paul also spoke of this when he asserted: ***The last enemy that shall be destroyed is death*** (I Corinthians 15:26).

The White Throne Judgment is the last outpouring of God's Wrath, and it will be released by the judgment of His Son Jesus Christ. Satan, his fallen angels, and all sin will have been removed from this earth. The earth itself will then be renovated by fire, and eternity will begin (II Peter 3:7, Malachi 4:1).

Judgment of the Antichrist, the False Prophet and Satan

Following the rapture of the church at the blowing of the 7th trumpet, the *seven bowls of God's wrath* will be poured out on the earth, and Satan, all of Satan's forces, the Antichrist and the False Prophet will be gathered to the *Battle of Armageddon* where all will be vanquished by Jesus Christ himself.

[11] *And I saw heaven opened, and behold a white horse; and he that sat upon him was called Faithful and True, and in righteousness he doth judge and make war.*
[12] *His eyes were as a flame of fire, and on his head were many crowns; and he had a name written, that no man knew, but he himself.*
[13] *And he was clothed with a vesture dipped in blood: and his name is called The Word of God.*
[14] *And the armies which were in heaven followed him upon white horses, clothed in fine linen, white and clean.*
[15] *And out of his mouth goeth a sharp sword, that with it he should smite the nations: and he shall rule them with a rod of iron: and he treads the winepress of the fierceness and wrath of Almighty God.*
[16] *And he hath on his vesture and on his thigh a name written, KING OF KINGS, AND LORD OF LORDS.*   Revelation 19:11-16

The battle will not last long. Zechariah recorded its outcome in graphic detail.

[1] *Behold, the day of the LORD cometh, and thy spoil shall be divided in the midst of thee.*
[2] *For I will gather all nations against Jerusalem to battle; and the city shall be taken, and the houses rifled, and the women ravished; and half of the city shall go forth into captivity, and the residue of the people shall not be cut off from the city.*
[3] *Then shall the LORD go forth, and fight against those nations, as when he fought in the day of battle.*

[4] And his feet shall stand in that day upon the mount of Olives, which is before Jerusalem on the east, and the mount of Olives shall cleave in the midst thereof toward the east and toward the west, and there shall be a very great valley; and half of the mountain shall remove toward the north, and half of it toward the south. Zechariah 14: 1-4

And this shall be the plague wherewith the LORD will smite all the people that have fought against Jerusalem; Their flesh shall consume away while they stand upon their feet, and their eyes shall consume away in their holes, and their tongue shall consume away in their mouth. Zechariah 14:12

When the battle is over, Christ will personally pass sentence upon the Antichrist (Revelation 13: 1-10) and the False Prophet (Revelation 13: 11-18). Both will be cast alive into the *lake of fire and brimstone*.

[19] And I saw the beast, and the kings of the earth, and their armies, gathered together to make war against him that sat on the horse, and against his army. [20] And the beast was taken, and with him the false prophet that wrought miracles before him, with which he deceived them that had received the mark of the beast, and them that worshipped his image. These both were cast alive into a lake of fire burning with brimstone. Revelation 19: 19-20

Satan will be cast into the bottomless pit, where he will be confined for 1000 years until the Millennial Kingdom has run its course. He will then return for one final battle (Revelation 20: 7-10c). After He has been defeated at the end of the Millennial Kingdom (Satan's Last Stand), he will join the Antichrist and the False Prophet in the *Lake of Fire and Brimstone*.

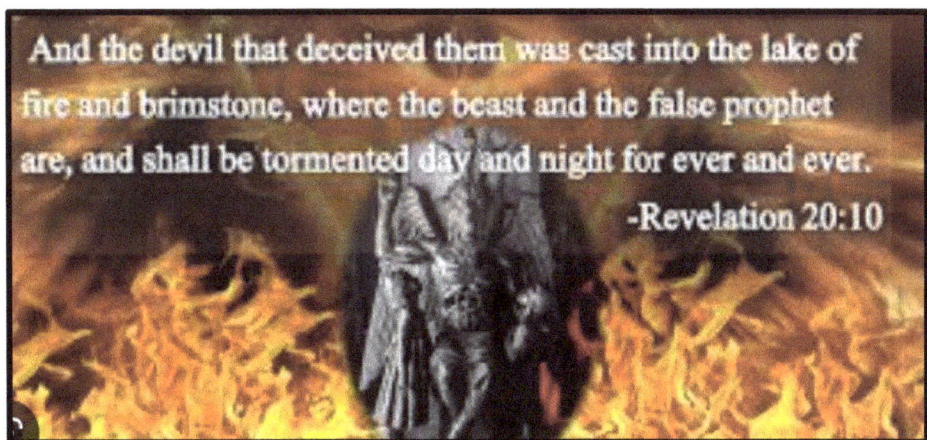

Bibliography

Coulter, Fred R., The Appointed Times of Jesus the Messiah, York Publishing Company, PO Box 1038, Hollister, California, 95024-1038

Dake, Finis J., Dake's Annotated Reference Bible, Dake Bible Sales, P.O. Box 1050, Lawrenceville, Ga., 30246

Finegan, Jack, Handbook of Biblical Chronology, Hendrickson Publishing Company, Peabody, Ma.

Good, Joseph, Rosh HaShanah and the Messianic Kingdom to Come, Hatikva Ministries, PO Box 3125, Port Arthur, Texas 77643-0703

Horn H. S. and L. H. Wood, The Chronology of Ezra, TEACH Services, Inc., www.teachservices.com

Larkin, Clarence, Dispensational Truth, P.O. Box 334, Glenside, Pa., 1920

Logos apostolic Church of God and Bible College, Interlinear Greek and Hebrew Translation, Logos apostolic.org, United Kingdom, Logos apostolic.org

Nee, Watchman, Come Lord Jesus, Christian Fellowship Publishers, Inc., 11515 Allecingie Parkway, Richmond, Virginia 23235

Phillips, Don T., The Book of Revelation: *Mysteries Revealed*, 2nd Edition, Virtual Bookworm. com, PO Box 9949, College Station, Texas 7784.

Phillips, Don T., The Book of Ruth: *Historical and Prophetic Truths*, Virtual Bookworm. com, PO Box 9949, College Station, Texas 7784.

Phillips, Don T., Life After Death: *Mysteries Revealed*, Virtual Bookworm. com, PO Box 9949, College Station, Texas 7784.

Phillips, Don T., The Eternal Plan of God: *Dispensations, Covenant Promises, Salvation*, Virtual Bookworm. com, PO Box 9949, College Station, Texas 7784.

Phillips, Don T., The Birth and Death of Christ, Virtual Bookworm. com, PO Box 9949, College Station, Texas 7784.

Phillips, Don T., The Book of Exodus: *Historical and Prophetic Truths* Virtual Bookworm. com, PO Box 9949, College Station, Texas 7784.

Phillips, Don T., A Biblical Chronology from Adam to Christ,

Virtual Bookworm. com, PO Box 9949, College Station, Texas 7784.

Phillips, Don T., Life After the Great Tribulation: *The Millennial Kingdom*
Virtual Bookworm. com, PO Box 9949, College Station, Texas 7784.

Phillips, Don T., The Last 50 Days of Jesus Christ
Virtual Bookworm. com, PO Box 9949, College Station, Texas 7784.

Phillips, Don T., The Daniel 70 Week Prophecy
Virtual Bookworm. com, PO Box 9949, College Station, Texas 7784.

Phillips, Don T., The Birth of Christ: A Forensic Analysis
Virtual Bookworm. com, PO Box 9949, College Station, Texas 7784.

Rosenthal, Matthew, The Pre-Wrath Rapture of the Church, Thomas Nelson Publishers, Nashville, Tennessee

Ryrie, Charles C., The Ryrie Study Bible, King James Version, Moody Press, Chicago

Salerno, Donald A., Revelation Unsealed, Virtual Bookworm.Com, P.O. Box 9949, College Station, Texas, 77842

Thiele, Edwin R., The Mysterious Numbers of the Hebrew Kings: Revised Edition, Kregel, Grand Rapids, Michigan

Thomas, Robert L., Revelation 1-7, An Exegetical Commentary, Moody Press, Chicago, Illinois

Thomas, Robert L., Revelation 8-22, An Exegetical Commentary, Moody Press, Chicago, Illinois

Van Kampen, Robert, The Sign, Crossway Books, 1300 Crescent Street, Wheaton, Illinois 60187

Walvoord, John F., The Millennial Kingdom, Academic Books, Zondervan Publishing Company, 1415 Lake Drive S.E., Grand Rapids, Michigan 49506

www.ingramcontent.com/pod-product-compliance
Lightning Source LLC
Chambersburg PA
CBHW042023180426
43200CB00034B/2992